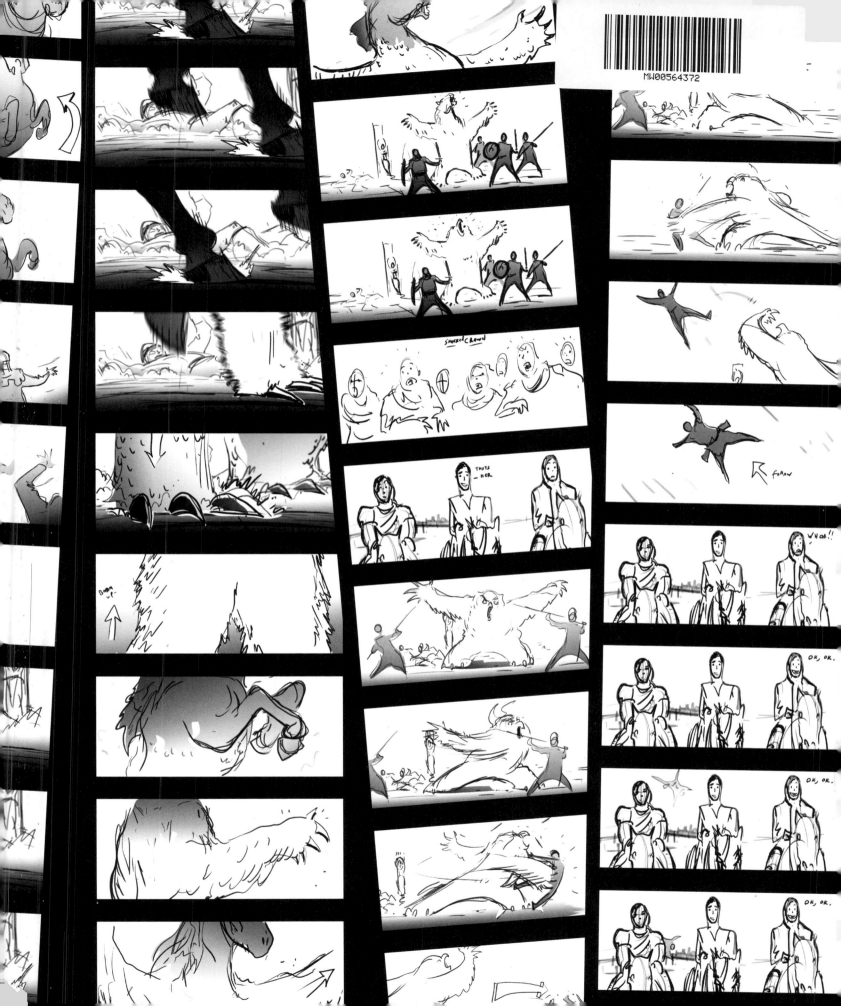

THE ART AND MAKING OF

DUNGEONS & DRAGONS®

HONOR AMONG THIEVES

THE ART AND MAKING OF

DUNGEONS & DRAGONS

HONOR AMONG THIEVES

WRITTEN BY ELENI ROUSSOS

Foreword by
John Francis Daley and
Jonathan Goldstein

TEN SPEED PRESS
California | New York

CONTENTS

FOREWORD

———◆◆◆———

A GAME OF D&D is in many ways similar to the process of filmmaking. You start in the prep phase, crafting your characters, plotting out your story, and equipping yourself with the best team possible. But the moment the campaign begins or the cameras start rolling, you realize that all your preparation only takes you so far, as the game—and the film—assume a life of their own. The challenges you couldn't have foreseen come rushing at you, whether it's a surprise attack by a horde of Gnolls or a Techno-crane breaking down on the morning of a three-page action sequence. And what you quickly come to realize is that pivoting is the point. How you adjust to what the world, or the Dungeon Master, throws your way determines your destiny. But contained in every hurdle is the potential to discover something you hadn't planned for at all. And sometimes those discoveries lead you to an even better path than all your preparation could have.

Here's an example: We ended shoot day 53 with a horseback "ride and talk" scene featuring Chris Pine and Michelle Rodriguez. With the sun setting and heavy rain moving in, we were racing against the clock. As we set up the shot, we quickly realized that because the camera truck was moving uphill, its engine noise overwhelmed our actors' dialogue. Loath to have to re-dub their lines later, we scrambled for a solution. That's when our line producer had the idea to change the direction of travel so that the truck could go silently downhill in neutral. It was a daunting prospect, as it required us to move the entire basecamp of tents and equipment 200 yards down the road in mere minutes. But there was no denying it was the best solution. The entire crew, including us, our producer, even studio execs chipped in to make the move. In that moment, job titles were irrelevant and the only thing that mattered was getting the shot. And as it turned out, the angle we ended up with was more striking than the one we had intended. That last-minute curveball made the movie better.

The freedom that D&D offers its players is exactly what made taking on a film adaptation so formidable. How do you represent in film form a game that is unique to its players, its characters and narrative constantly evolving? The answer for us was that the movie had to capture that distinctive feeling you get when playing the game. The constant interweaving of life-and-death stakes with laugh-out-loud absurdity. And, of course, the magic and monsters derived from fifty years of lore. But as with any good campaign, we couldn't embark on this adventure alone. The book you're about to read showcases the development and painstaking work of some of the most talented artists, designers, and technicians in their field. Spanning a period of over three years, we worked hand-in-hand with hundreds of these visionaries to literally create a world. Our hope is that this book and the film that inspired it will offer you a glimpse of the magic that D&D has given us and the millions of others fortunate enough to have enjoyed it.

—John Francis Daley & Jonathan Goldstein

INTRODUCTION

SINCE THE 1970S, the game DUNGEONS & DRAGONS has been delighting fans with its unique blend of fantasy-genre roleplay and creative storytelling. From humble beginnings, it has grown into the bestselling tabletop roleplaying game in the United States. The game has made its way into countless areas of popular culture, from books and comics to video games and toys to an animated series, and, of course, film. D&D now has millions of fans worldwide, including the co-directors and writers for the film *Dungeons & Dragons: Honor Among Thieves*, Jonathan Goldstein and John Francis Daley. "John and I both [have] been longtime fans and players of DUNGEONS & DRAGONS the game, so when the opportunity came to us to, at first, rewrite and then direct the motion picture version of it, we were very excited," says Goldstein. "It's a world that allows so much potential because the game itself is so immersive and has so much creative freedom for the players. We wanted to bring the experience of playing the game onto the screen as best we could."

"What was so fun about it was that sense of sheer freedom," Daley recalls of the first time he played DUNGEONS & DRAGONS. "You're only confined by the very basic rules of the game, but beyond that, you can decide to do anything you want to as a character. And I thought that there was something so liberating in that. And so, when the option to make this movie came to us, we jumped at it because it allowed for us to capture that magic that we felt playing it."

Their own experiences playing the game meant that the filmmakers were uniquely prepared for the challenge of bringing DUNGEONS & DRAGONS to the big screen. "The overall appeal is taking something that people know and love, and using that as a platform to create a great story in a fantasy world that is fully realized," states producer Jeremy Latcham. "DUNGEONS & DRAGONS is one of the most enduring pieces of

American pop culture and being able to tell a story in that world is a real privilege. And it's something that weighs heavily on us because we want to get it right, and we want to make sure that it's done properly."

The game itself is quite intricate, both in its game mechanics and in its world design. "It's complicated," says Latcham. "It's full of lore and rules and different classes and cultures and all kinds of different settings, and it's a really complex world. And so, to take that and to translate it, it's a huge responsibility for the guys, and to take something that's so iconic and revered and loved by so many fans around the world, it's a really large task."

To aid in the endeavor, the filmmakers collaborated with Wizards of the Coast, the current game publishers for DUNGEONS & DRAGONS. "Early in the process, we traveled up to Seattle to spend some time with the Wizards of the Coast at their offices up there," continues Goldstein. "It was a really unique experience, because we got to hear from the horse's mouth, if you will, what works and what they had some issues with."

"They were so helpful in bolstering some of the plot pieces that may, or may not have, fit into the lore, and making them all work in a natural way," adds Daley.

The Wizards team was an ever-present resource to the filmmakers, making sure to answer any questions, or provide creative suggestions regarding the game's content and intellectual property as it was applied to the film. "As we're taking IP from the games and bringing them into new mediums, I like to say, 'We're not looking for accuracy, we *are* looking for authenticity,'" explains Jeremy Jarvis, senior creative director, Wizards Franchise Development. "And so, creative liberties can be taken if it's not that important, or it's too much fun to pass up. And you really want to spend [time] where it *is* important, but finding those moments of authenticity of, like, 'Yes.

This is plausible. This feels right,' even if you're taking creative liberties. Because creative liberties have to be taken as you are engaging in new mediums and new expressions."

"We've had a great amount of support from our friends at Wizards of the Coast, who've been nothing but stellar advocates for the lore, for the movie—to make sure we all do it right," Latcham comments. "Hopefully, with all of us collaborating so closely, we create something that feels true to everybody, and can bring new fans along, and delight old fans as well."

"I'll be frank—I have never played DUNGEONS & DRAGONS," executive producer Denis L. Stewart says. "I've never been a board game—or any sort of role-playing game—guy, but I will tell you that Jeremy, John, and Jonathan . . . were always checking themselves with respect to the genesis of this genre. Of this force that is DUNGEONS & DRAGONS. They always paid great respect to it. And that's the complication of writing anything comedic about something that is as near and dear to millions of peoples' hearts. They worked really, really, really hard to respect that, but at the same time, not make something that was a trope, or that you would expect to see."

Knowing there would be two types of audience members in the future—those who have played the game before, and those who haven't—filmmakers had to strike a balance to ensure everyone could both understand and enjoy it. "Making a movie like this is always walking a line from a filmmaking perspective, because you have to bring in the people who don't know much about the IP, while satisfying those who do," Goldstein elaborates. "And that was very much in our minds every day of shooting this thing. How do we not alienate those, like my mom, who doesn't know anything about D&D, to the hardcore fans, you know? And so, it's really about walking that line."

Striking that balance wasn't the only challenge the filmmakers faced. Early in preproduction—the first phase of filmmaking before cameras start to roll—the COVID-19 pandemic began, greatly affecting the project's logistics and development. "There were a lot of challenges from a physical production standpoint," recalls Latcham. "Trying to mount a movie this big, and to launch something this iconic in [the] middle of COVID, is complicated in its own right. You're talking about not getting to meet your actors [in person] until Day One [of the shoot]. You're talking about not getting to meet your crew until after you've hired them and [have] been working with them for months. And so, you're dealing with a lot of people on little, itty bitty Zoom boxes from all kinds of different time zones, and trying to piece that together and make a film in the midst of that is a challenge in its own right."

"Throughout it all, we only lost two days of shooting due to COVID," Stewart adds. "It was because we really dug in and implemented a close contact tracing system, and we were doing the testing regimen that was prescribed by the unions and the studios. When someone tested positive, we could immediately isolate them and then quickly determine and ascertain who they had been in close contact with, and it allowed us to keep our crew moving around to continue to shoot the movie. It was a lot of work and it was really hard. . . . Making movies during COVID is exhausting."

"I think COVID certainly, it's just a bad disease," says Daley. "It's really bad in every way, and even in the most trivial way of trying to make a movie. It makes everything ten times more difficult—between the rigorous and very strict testing procedures that they do, and isolating people—which is all, obviously, necessary, but also makes it really difficult to establish that familial mentality that you want to have on a set. And fortunately, we have such a great group here that we established it regardless of what we were all up against, and that made it all the more triumphant of a moment to get here."

The filmmakers hope the film can bring a bit of brightness to what has otherwise been, for many, a time of struggle and hardship. "As this movie comes together, we're going to see all kinds of stuff," Latcham remarks. "We're going to see spectacular action, we're going to see great character work, we're going to see incredible humor, and we're going to see a friendship being born between a group of people as a team that becomes a family. And to me, those are the most resonant themes in cinema—a group of people becoming a family. Family is this thing I think we need more of now than ever in the world."

"We cared a great deal—not just about executing the script we'd written—but creating something that's worthy of D&D," states Goldstein. "There's a reason it's been around and so enormously popular, and I don't think there's been a television show or a movie or anything that has done it justice yet. And we really set out to do that. And that meant digging deep into the lore. Having someone on set who could really tell us, 'Is there a verbal component to this spell? And what do they have to do with their hands?' All that little detail stuff. We took liberties where we had to, because we weren't shooting a game, we were shooting a movie, and sometimes you have to make those changes, but hopefully it will come across in the watching [of the film] that we cared a lot, and we love this game, and hopefully we've done it right."

"Going into this, we were not the sort of cynical, commercial directors trying to get a cash grab out of the beloved franchise," adds Daley. "We understand what it is that makes D&D so special, and why in my mind it is a game that can, and I don't mean this lightly, change the world—in that it's the only one that promotes boundless creativity in people that wouldn't necessarily consider themselves creative. It isn't just the [Dungeon Master] that's telling the stories. It's all the players as well. And what D&D allows you to do is enter this storytelling space in a very organic way that you don't even realize you're coming up with ideas and being a creative storyteller until after you've told it. And that to me is a magic trick. And the idea of being able to show that in the film space, and really capture the essence of that feeling, was something we took incredibly seriously, and knew that we couldn't screw up. So, hopefully that also translates to non-players. We did try to make it as approachable to all audiences as we could, but we definitely knew, at its core, this is as D&D of a film that we could ever make."

emerald
enclave
brooch

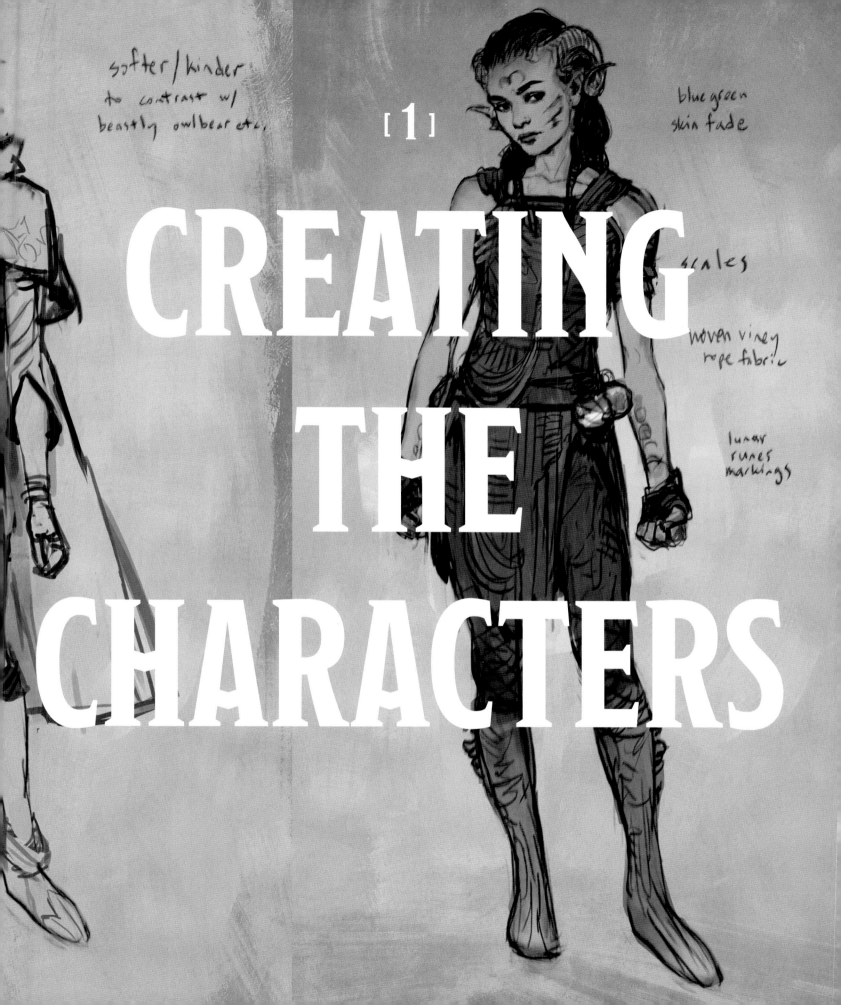

softer/kinder
to contrast w/
beastly owlbear etc.

blue green
skin fade

scales

woven viney
rope fabric

lunar
runes
markings

CREATING THE CHARACTERS

THE ADVENTURING PARTY

SITTING DOWN TO play a game of DUNGEONS & DRAGONS, the first thing you must decide is what character to play. Limited only by your imagination, you develop your adventurer's appearance, personality, and backstory. Perhaps you decide to play as an overconfident gnomish fighter who believes he can take on the largest of beasts single-handedly, or an elderly dwarven bard desperate for the celebrity he once held in his youth. The characteristics you choose will become the starting point for every decision you make in your game. Thrown into the world, you meet up with other adventurers like yourself, and get thrust into an epic campaign where anything can happen.

The filmmakers went through similar steps when choosing what characters to create for the movie. "[We] approached it from the standpoint you would if you were starting a campaign in the game of D&D," co-director and writer Jonathan Goldstein explains. "It was important to us to create characters who feel relatable, even though they're of another time and they're in another world. They feel like they could be representative of the kids, or adults, who are playing the game in a lot of ways."

Once your character is chosen, you take on that role, portraying their actions and personality through your gameplay. You verbalize your decisions and interact with other characters in the way that *you* decide best represents your adventurer. Maybe your character speaks with an accent, or only in rhyme. Perhaps your character is stricken with fear whenever they smell smoked foods because they are reminded of their childhood village burning down. Whatever your choices are, you can guarantee they will be unique to you.

The actors chosen to portray the adventuring party in the film ended up being as diverse as their characters. "The casting process is always complicated," producer Jeremy Latcham reflects. "When you're creating new characters that you hope are going to be around for a long time, you want to spend all the time to make sure you get exactly the right people, and I think we've really done that."

Opposite the adventuring players, the DM, or Dungeon Master, details out the world that you will find yourself in and sets up the various challenges your group will face. The DM is responsible for orchestrating the circumstances that bring everyone together. Perhaps while chartering a boat to distant shores, you're set upon by pirates. Perhaps everyone just happens to be drinking in the same tavern when one sharp insult devolves into an all-out brawl. While the initiation of a campaign is not always simple or straightforward, it prompts the adventurers to come together, loosely aligned toward a common goal.

For this film, several central characters were entwined by a united backstory. "Our main cast of characters are a band of thieves," says co-director and writer John Francis Daley. "And the thing that separates them from bad guys is that they uphold this sense of nobility and honor among themselves. They are not *bad* guys. They want to do good, and they have turned to thieving for their own reasons, but ultimately have veered toward the path of getting the job done in saving the land." Concept artist and character lead Wes Burt set out with this design brief to craft a visual style for our so-called team of heroes.

EDGIN

EDGIN DARVIS

Brazen and charismatic, the human Edgin Darvis is the former leader of a band of thieves. "He is a charmer," describes Daley. "He is a fast thinker. He's a planner and a storyteller. And I think his real superpower is getting people on board with far-fetched plans."

"He thinks all of his plans work wonderfully," Latcham states of Edgin's schemes. "They rarely ever work. And that's what makes him such a lovable guy because he keeps trying and trying and trying."

Edgin blamed himself for his wife's death after a plan to provide a better life for his family went awry, and subsequently turned to a life of crime. Convinced to go after one last score, Edgin is arrested, convicted, and sent to a prison called Revel's End to serve out his sentence. Isolated in his prison cell, Edgin thinks only of his young daughter, Kira, and how to reunite with her once again. "We wanted a bit of an antihero in Edgin," Daley explains. "He is kind of selfish and greedy when we first meet him. He went to jail for being a thief, and he learns his way over the course of the film, and in [actor] Chris Pine, we found that perfect blend of likability, but also mischief."

"Chris is one of the few actors who can do both comedy and emotion equally well, and that's an elusive trait when you're casting a movie like this," adds Goldstein. "So, we've been very happy with everything he's given us because he delivered on both those fronts."

It was easy for Pine to be drawn to the character of Edgin Darvis. "It reminds me of Harrison [Ford] and Indiana [Jones]. . . . It reminds me of Bruce Willis in *Die Hard*. It reminds me of all my favorite actors growing up. They're just very normal, and they can be very, very scared just like everybody else and I like that about Edgin. He's got a fair dose of being absolutely terrified by things, and he can be a big baby and selfish and rude, but he's trying," Pine remarks.

Edgin is a *bard*, a class of individuals who are masterful orators and skillful in song. They are also users of magic. A classic bard special ability in DUNGEONS & DRAGONS is called *bardic inspiration*—inspiring others with empowering words or music—something viewers can see Edgin do often during the film. "He is undeniably an optimist," Pine says of his character. "He will make the best out of any situation, and I guess from the definitions from DUNGEONS & DRAGONS, getting the bard is the inspirer. The bard is the one that inspires hope and courage and people to do their best. And so, when you first meet Edgin, he's knitting a pair of mittens for his daughter, Kira, who he hopes to be seeing. He is reveling in the undoubted escape that will happen. And even when he's chopping ice, he's singing and trying to get his compatriots, who are miserable and soon to die awful deaths, into a group singalong."

While many different instruments can be used by bards, Edgin plays a lute that is also reinforced for close-range combat. "We had the idea of using a pipa—also known as a Chinese lute—for inspiration," recalls set decorator Naomi Moore. "The shape seemed really elegant, and a fresh change from the usual English-style medieval shapes usually seen in movies. We then worked through interesting ways that Edgin might have armored it as a weapon. As tortoises seem to feature within the D&D world, we made panels that looked like they could be a shell attached with leather and studding on the back. Once the concept was approved, we then had to work out how to actually translate the design into a three-dimensional object that could actually be played. Miraculously, it turned out that Jake Menear, one of our local carpenters, had actually made guitars for a living previously and was somewhat of an expert in how to turn a piece of wood into a beautiful, working, stringed instrument."

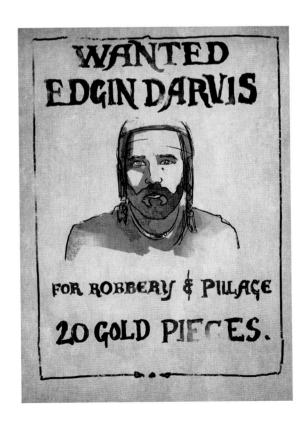

WANTED
EDGIN DARVIS

FOR ROBBERY & PILLAGE

20 GOLD PIECES.

HOLGA

HOLGA KILGORE

Human barbarian Holga Kilgore is as forceful as they come. A once proud member of the Uthgardt Elk Tribe, she was banished from her clan for falling in love with an outsider. Although Holga married the man of her dreams, she grew despondent due to the loss of her clan, which put a strain on the marriage. Eventually their relationship crumbled and she found herself all alone.

Wandering the land, Holga soon finds herself in a new tribe of sorts, becoming the first recruit to Edgin's band of thieves. "When you're shunned by the world and you find acceptance somewhere, it's a beautiful thing," actor Michelle Rodriguez asserts. "I would cherish that and take care of it and make sure that I'm very gentle in how I treat that relationship. And so, I think that's kind of Holga's thing [now] that she's been shunned by her tribe, and she finds a new team. A new place to belong."

Arrested alongside Edgin during a failed robbery, Holga is also sent to Revel's End to serve out her sentence, but she remains confident that Edgin will come up with a plan to get them out. Holga has a deep bond with Edgin, but that doesn't extend to romance. "She's not the love interest in the movie, which is a departure from what you normally see in these kind of fantasy films," Goldstein remarks of Holga. "She's more of a sister to Edgin, and a real tough character in her own right."

"She doesn't talk much in the beginning," Rodriguez states of her character. "She doesn't really like to talk much in general, which I like. I really enjoyed that about her. I like people of few words. But when she does say something, she could say it with her fist, or maybe her feet, or her eyes. . . . She's definitely a presence."

Don't let Holga's intensity fool you, however. She has a sweet spot for both Edgin's daughter, Kira, and for the taste of raw potatoes. "In Michelle Rodriguez, we found such an amazing and interesting blend of that stoicism, but also this goofiness—this inherent goofiness that Michelle exudes in the most incredible way," claims Daley. "She's just been an absolute delight to work with, and one of the most unique actors that I've ever had the pleasure of working with, as well."

Holga is a *barbarian*, a class of warriors who, if triggered in combat, can be consumed by a primal brutality. In the world of DUNGEONS & DRAGONS, this is known as *rage*. When raging, they deal increased damage, making a barbarian particularly dangerous to all who stand within an arm's, or blade's, reach of them. "They don't have magic," explains Rodriguez. "Their biggest power is pretty much their passionate fury."

Holga triggers her rage by slapping herself before heading into the fray. "Holga is a terrific fighter and we get to see her barbarian rage come into play several times in the film," Goldstein shares.

Holga wears the traditional garb of her clan. To design this look, the filmmakers sought inspiration from ancient Earthly civilizations. "The Holga outfit is beautiful," Rodriguez says of her costume. "It conjures up all these ideas of these different types of ancient warriors from different cultures. Like, I get Mongol vibes when I see the whole outfit together, but you could see the Viking influence with the shield in the front, in the top, and a lot of the padding that's leather-bound and the boots and stuff."

Holga's arms are also covered in tattoos and branding scars, permanent reminders of her past as a member of the Uthgardt Elk Tribe.

For most of the film, Holga wields a greataxe. It has a telescoping handle and is forged with darksteel by famed D&D dwarven mastersmith Ghelryn Foehammer. "We have probably about ten different variants on the shaft because the shaft extends," explains weapons master Tommy Dunne of Holga's greataxe. "You're able to lengthen the shaft [to] small or big, depending on your fight action. So, even that alone there's, like, ten different variants on the handle."

Like most weapons seen onscreen, several different versions were created for filming. While some were heavy and made of various metals, others were made with safety in mind. "You have the soft head so we can actually hit each other," adds Dunne. "You'd have all soft—soft handles, [and] soft heads—for on horseback [to] make sure that the horses never have any trouble with it—and also then for the actor, regarding them, [to] make sure if they ever come off the horse that they'd have a soft landing."

SIMON

SIMON AUMAR

Simon is a *sorcerer*, a spellcaster class that is chosen by birthright. Although a descendant of famed wizard Elminster Aumar, half-elf Simon Aumar is mediocre when it comes to magic. "We wanted a less-than-perfect version of a sorcerer," Goldstein notes. "Normally in movies, you see the guy or girl who really knows what they're doing. And so, Simon is someone who comes from a very esteemed family lineage, and that's a lot of pressure on him like anybody who comes from a family where your parents, your grandparents, were great at something and you're not. So, he has to deal with that on a daily basis. And in [actor] Justice Smith, we got a great version of that. He's self-deprecating and he's very vulnerable."

Simon was part of the original band of thieves with Edgin and Holga. During the team's failed robbery attempt, Simon manages to avoid capture. With his compatriots in prison, Simon now gets by as a solo act, pulling off lesser crimes using minor magics. "[He] is riddled with insecurity about his magic most likely because he is a descendant of wizarding blood and of a great sorcerer," Smith says of his character. "He can't really live up to that pressure, nor to the pressure of being a descendant of magical experts, and so he has internalized that he is never going to be enough and just bathes in his own self-deprecation and has resorted to just using his tricks for petty thievery."

Eventually, Edgin and Holga seek out Simon when they escape from Revel's End. Edgin is in need of a sorcerer and he's confident that Simon's abilities have improved over the last two years. Although Edgin is quickly proven wrong, Simon does learn to be a more confident magic user by the end of the movie. "Over the course of the film, he discovers that inner fire inside of himself and finally wields the power that he always had, but never, never knew he did," shares Daley.

Sorcerers derive power through their bloodline, which makes them different from other magic users. "Wizards are more academic, studious," explains Smith. "They basically start from a place of non-magic, and then study and acquire magical abilities. Sorcerers are born with magical abilities, and often they are triggered by some sort of catastrophic event in their life, or emotion, or a variety of things. For Simon, he is a sorcerer of wild magic, which means that often when he's trying to do a spell, something other than what he intended will happen, so his life is chaotic."

In DUNGEONS & DRAGONS, some sorcerers possess an innate ability to wield an uncontrolled magic known as *wild magic*. Their power is derived from the forces of chaos, and for every non-cantrip spell, there is a chance that a surge of untamed magic will be released. While there is a chance that something good can sprout from wild magic, more often than not, the sorcerer is left wanting. "The thing that I find beautiful about Simon is that he's not necessarily upset that he's not good at magic," Smith continues. "He really has come to terms with it, which is why he makes himself a butt of jokes. It definitely is his obstacle. Throughout the story [he] is trying to come into his own power, but I love the idea of someone who's just kind of practical about where they're at, and not in a 'woe is me' kind of way—just in a 'this is how I am and I accept that' kind of way."

Simon Aumar carries a variety of material components to help with his spellcasting. "For certain spells, you need a somatic element, a verbal element, and you need a material element," explains Smith. "So, John and Jonathan took that into account and gave Simon a magic dispenser that basically, I think, has all sort of materials in it and you just have to twist it and it releases those materials."

Simon obtains a few additional artifacts during the party's adventure. A basic walking stick that Holga had once gifted her ex-husband ends up back in her possession. This wooden staff turns out to be a *hither-thither staff*—an item that allows the user to open two portals within sight no more than 500 yards apart. This allows the wielder of the staff, and anyone with them, to easily traverse large distances.

Another magical item obtained is called the *helm of disjunction*. Once a sorcerer attunes to it, that wearer can disable all nearby enchantments. "The helm is incredibly powerful and needs to be kept safe so it does not fall into the wrong hands," conveys actor Regé-Jean Page, whose character knows where it is hidden.

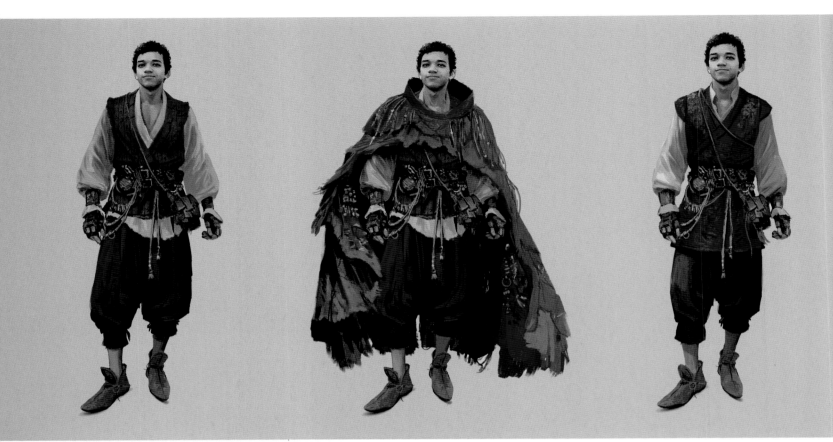

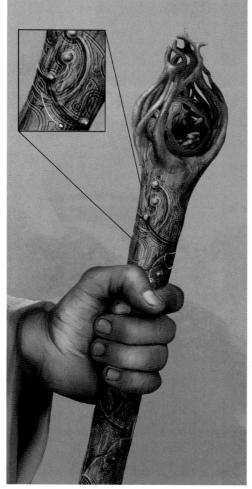

DORIC

LC

DORIC

When Edgin needs someone to sneak into a castle to get intel, he suggests to Holga and Simon that they add a *druid* to the team—someone who can use the *wild shape* ability to transform into a beast. Druids are a class of individuals who have a strong bond with animals and nature. Their added ability to turn into a wild shape means they can transform into a wide variety of beasts. In DUNGEONS & DRAGONS, this ability is limited to creatures the druid has seen before. This trait comes in useful not only for combat but also for exploration and other tasks.

Edgin is hopeful that a small mouse will be able to scurry past guards undetected. Enter Doric. "She's played by [actor] Sophia Lillis and she is also a wild shape," Goldstein says of the druid. "So, we get to see her use that power in the movie where she can turn into any number of animals."

Turning into animals isn't Doric's only talent. "Doric is a tiefling, and unlike the rest of our gang, she is pretty good at everything that she does and sets out to do," observes Daley. "She lives by a code of ethics. She's not a thief, and she's, in many ways, the outlier in the group."

Doric is a member of the Emerald Enclave, a faction of individuals that believes in the natural order of all things—like the balance between nature and civilization, or good and evil—and are against anything that upsets this balance. Doric was raised with these beliefs from a young age. "She was born from humans, but they abandoned her," reveals Lillis. "So she was taken in by the wood elves, and she was brought up [with them] and tries to do whatever she can to protect them. . . . She doesn't quite fit though even though they respect her because of what she does. She's not really like them. So she always felt kind of off, but she would do whatever she can to protect them because they helped her when she was a kid."

These beliefs drive Doric's decision to join the team. "She doesn't want to work with them specifically," suggests Lillis of Edgin's newly formed group, "but she also knows she would do whatever she can to save her family. To save her home."

Doric is also a *tiefling*, a type of character in DUNGEONS & DRAGONS that, although primarily human, share a lineage with infernal beings such as a demon, succubus, or evil deity. Because of this heritage, some people are distrustful of them, although this ancestry has no bearing on whether a tiefling is "good" or "evil." You can identify a tiefling by their horns and prehensile tail. Some tieflings also have colored skin, like red, green, or purple—and can even have additional physical traits such as wings, scales, or hooves—while others can almost pass for human.

The filmmakers ultimately gravitated toward a more natural-looking tiefling with softer edges for Doric's final look. "Doric was my favorite, because it's a little girl, pretty girl, with this kind of horn," hair and makeup designer Alessandro Bertolazzi reveals. "[We wanted it] to be natural, attractive, beautiful, and fancy and nice and sweet at the same time. I think we got that."

It was important to the filmmakers that Doric's horns be shot practically, meaning they would be filmed on set—not added later by computer effects. As such, artisans had to devise a way for these bodily attachments to be applied not only in easy and efficient ways but also be safe for filming. "I really thought it was completely genius, what they did," Lillis discloses of her horns' application. "I had basically a cap on that had two little nubs that were magnets, and then over on top [of that] I had a wig. And they plucked on the two horns that fit into those magnet holes. . . . The only issue is that when I do my rolls and everything, those immediately pop off. So that was the one kind of nervous, you know, one little issue when I start doing all of this stuff—and especially with fight scenes—where they have just one shot of everybody and then [the camera] going to me and I do one roll, and both of them just go flying, you know? So, I was very nervous about that, but it actually worked out really well in the end."

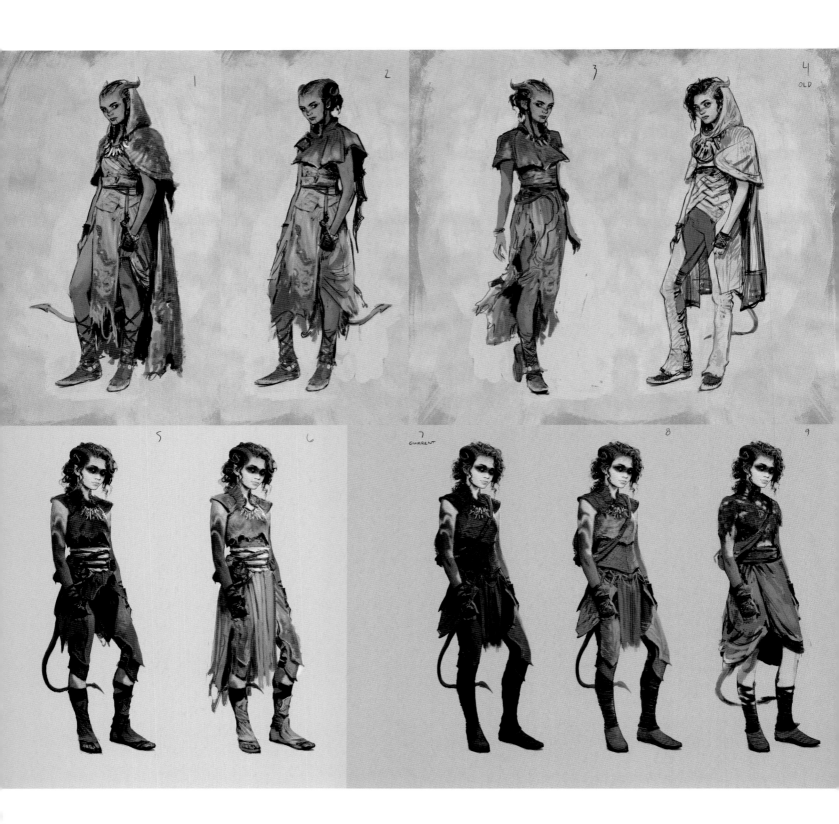

The Emerald Enclave

Deep in the Neverwinter Wood, the tiefling Doric lives among other members of the Emerald Enclave—like druids and rangers. Often those with a deep connection to nature choose to become members. "[Doric] was adopted," reiterates Latcham. "She was abandoned. She was left on the side of the road by humans, and adopted by wood elves that kindly took her in, and it is now her holy quest to live up to their expectations, and to return the favor they have done for her. She joined the Emerald Enclave to protect her adoptive family."

"The members of the Emerald Enclave have structured and armored clothing, more similar to Doric, to signal their role as the fighters and defenders of the druids," says costume designer Amanda Monk.

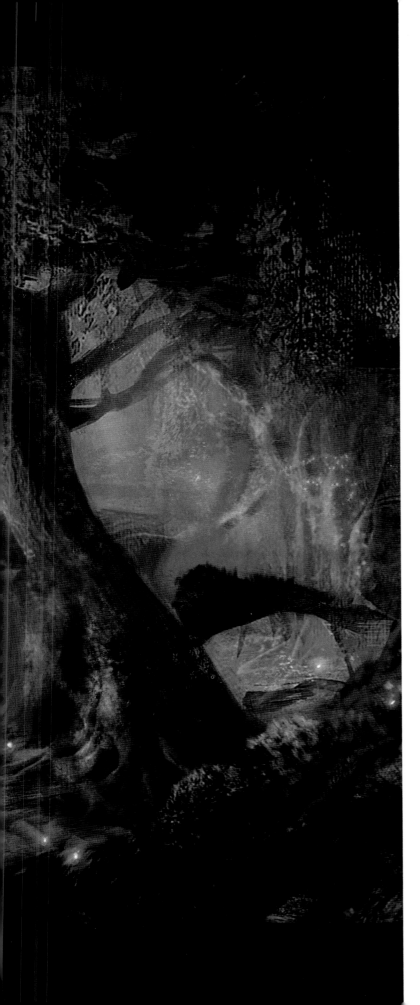

THOSE MET ALONG THE WAY

WHEN YOU PLAY a game of DUNGEONS & DRAGONS, you interact with more characters than just the ones in your adventuring party. The DM decides which nonplayer characters, or NPCs, you will meet and how they'll interact with you (and even acts them out for you during the game). These NPCs help build your world—from selling you items to giving you quests. It is these interactions that propel the campaign forward in new and exciting directions.

Something similar happens in filmmaking. Instead of a DM bringing these NPCs to life, the directors and producers work with other departments on the film—like costumes, special effects, and prosthetics—to help develop a cohesive vision and backstory for all the characters seen onscreen. "Every movie has a different vibe, every movie a different story," says hair and makeup designer Alessandro Bertolazzi. "Anything we do needs a story behind it. Every single character, every single tattoo. Even a scar. Even a wound. Everything needs a story. Without story, nothing's going to be [feel] real."

The world and lore of DUNGEONS & DRAGONS is vast, but, like the game, there is always room for creativity. "You have much more scope to play around with and to react to as well," asserts Dunne. "You're not stuck within a genre where a historian will go, 'That was never invented and that was never around.' We have, basically, a blank canvas to make and design within the world."

ZIA DARVIS

In the fishing village of Targos, a young Edgin Darvis is married to a woman named Zia. Although they are without riches, they are content. Soon the couple becomes a family of three, and their happiness grows even more. But Edgin's feelings of jubilation are marred by burden. With another mouth to feed, Edgin desires to give his family more than his meager earnings allow. So, when a chance arises for him to steal some gold he believes will not be missed, he seizes the opportunity. Unfortunately, these coins are marked by magic, leading the money's original owners straight to Edgin's doorstep.

Alone at home and apprehensive about a sudden and strange arrival, Zia hides her infant as a precaution. Unfortunately for poor Zia, she does not stand a chance against the vengeful visitors. Later, when Edgin comes home, he sees what has been done beneath his roof. His wife has been murdered, and all for his self-ishness. Overcome with grief, he blames himself for her untimely death.

His guilt does not subside. Even ten years later, Edgin decides to lead his band of thieves on a risky heist once he learns of a chance to correct his past mistake. The vault they are tasked to break into contains a *tablet of reawakening*—a magical artifact that can bring any deceased person back to life. Edgin believes that if he gets hold of this tablet, he can give his daughter her mother back, and have Zia back in his arms. "One of the most important pivotal parts of being a human, or an animal, alive on this planet is bringing life into the world and protecting that life, and nurturing it," Pine observes. "This battle between our selfish natures and our selfless better natures for the group is what Edgin is battling. And the pain of having lost the great love of his life, the great over-whelming desire to bring that love back, the hard choice of putting that desire to bed, and doing the right thing."

KIRA DARVIS

Though Edgin and Holga are only friends, they raise Kira together after Zia's tragic death. "She lost her mother at a young age, but she had Edgin and Holga, who was like her mother figure," actor Chloe Coleman says of her character. "That was one of the biggest parts of her life, Holga being there. It meant the world to her because she grew really close with her and they had this connection that I really loved, that Kira and Holga have, because she looks up to her. She admires Holga a lot."

Holga is equally fond of young Kira and gives Kira what becomes her most prized possession. "It's this really pretty golden invisibility pendant and it has this green gemstone in the middle," Coleman explains. "When I tap it, I become invisible for as long as I want until I tap it again. I've had it ever since I was really young. It was one of the first things that Holga stole for me. . . . Kira never takes it off. It's one of her favorite things."

Edgin and Holga attempt a risky heist, but they are caught and arrested. With both of them behind bars, Kira ends up in the care of a rogue named Forge Fitzwilliam. "He gives me the idea that Edgin and Holga are these bad, greedy people—these bandits who left me for money," Coleman reveals. "She thinks that Edgin and Holga don't love her and it confuses her and it hurts her deeply. And even [though] Edgin and Holga come back, the moment that they do, [they] leave again. It leaves her even more distraught and she feels like everything has been taken away from her and she doesn't understand. She's confused and upset."

Of course, Edgin and Holga didn't abandon Kira— they were double-crossed and captured, but they never stop trying to find a way back to Kira. "Both Holga and Edgin have a profound love for little Kira," Rodriguez maintains. "Edgin, because that's his child, and Holga because she just really loves the kid. She's known her for many years, and saw her grow up and really cares for her. And so, I think that is what drives them through the whole story."

Kira is distrustful of her absentee father, so reestablishing the familial relationship won't be easy. "[He's] lost his daughter and made great mistakes about raising his child, and he's learning from that," says Pine.

FORGE FITZWILLIAM

FORGE FITZWILLIAM

"Never put your trust in a con man." Confident and dapper, Forge Fitzwilliam uses his charisma to disarm unsuspecting individuals. "Forge has always fancied himself as a ladies' man," actor Hugh Grant claims of his character. "He's managed to open doors through his charm, and insouciance, and fake aristocracy. And I think part of that was having rather beautiful hair and having dashing costumes."

"The inspiration for Forge's character was a medieval version of a vain, aging rockstar," recalls costume designer Amanda Monk. "A dandy with high aspirations. He wore a signature neckerchief, rings, a medallion, and a statement belt buckle."

Having Hugh Grant in the film was a dream come true for both Goldstein and Daley, who conceived the role of Forge specifically for the actor. "Hugh Grant was a real get for us," recalls Goldstein. "He was exactly who we wrote the part for. Hugh was just so perfect and so funny—[he] brought so much of his own charm and rakishness to the thing, it really brought the character to life. He told us, when we first Zoomed with him, he said that he hates everything he reads and he loved this script. He asked his agent which of us was British because he felt it so captured the British sensibility and sense of humor, which is not a surprise because we're both raised on Monty Python and the absurdity, and the intelligent stupidity of those movies, if you will."

Forge is a human *rogue,* a class of individuals in DUNGEONS & DRAGONS that is composed mainly of thieves, assassins, and tricksters. Rogues can make an honest living, but most fall on the wrong side of traditional law and order. While rogues are handy with a blade, they generally rely on their stealth and wits to get them out of troublesome situations, though some rogues—known as *arcane tricksters*—can even use magic.

As a professional scoundrel, it's only natural for Forge to antagonize the main heroes. "[Forge] is one of the baddies in the movie," Goldstein discloses. "He used to be a member of the group of thieves that Edgin and Holga and the rest were associated with. He left them early in the movie, and when we pick up a couple years later, we find that he is now the Lord of Neverwinter."

"The difference in the costume from rogue to Lord [of] Neverwinter was within the fabrics and color, becoming somewhat bolder, more ostentatious—cottons to silks," adds Monk. "Jewelry, once noble, were made of precious metals and gems. His color palette incorporated more gold and jewel tones whilst he still retained many of his signature pieces from his earlier days."

Forge's sudden rise to power confuses Edgin and Holga. "We shot the introduction of Forge Fitzwilliam, Hugh Grant's character, and when we first meet him, he is this inviting, warm, vibrant character," Daley notes. "That takes our guys aback because they don't quite know what to make of him. They don't know how he became the Lord of Neverwinter, or what he did to get there. And then, as we learn very quickly, he's still a bastard."

Despite Fitzwilliam's being a scoundrel, Grant conveyed the character's roguish ways to perfection. "We like our villains to have nuance and layers to them, and what Hugh Grant brought to the table was this inherent charm and likability that he just can't get rid of," Daley continues. "It flows out of him, even in his most miserable moments."

"There's always a key garment with every character," maintains Grant. "For me, the key garment is his neckerchief. He wears these little cravats that he ties here, and he has them whether he's an impoverished thief or whether he's a Lord of Neverwinter, or even at the end when he's in prison. You can't take it away from him. It's like his dummy—his comforter—and it's his reminder [of] when he was a dashing young man and women fell at his feet."

gold tooth, scar   hair

hair sideburns 3   hair/moustache 4, scar, goldtooth   longhair ponytail 5, scar, goldtooth

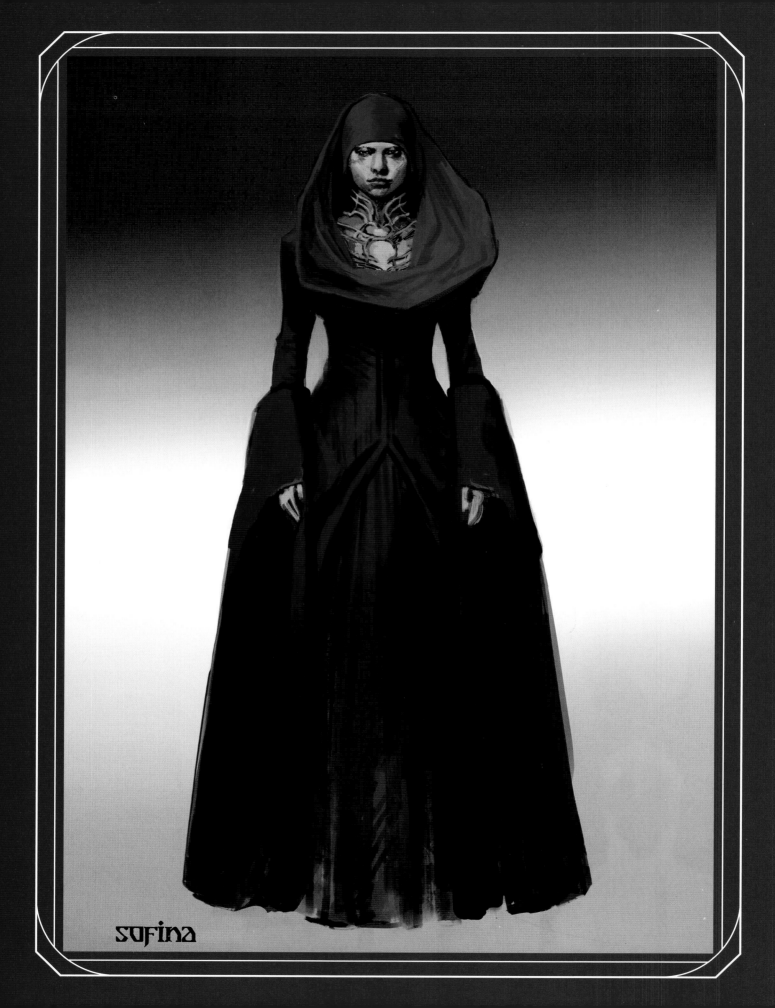

SUFINA

SOFINA

A mysterious human, Sofina hides her true identity as a Red Wizard. "Red Wizards are the ruling class of Thay, and their leader, their ruler, is Szass Tam," says actor Daisy Head. "They are ultimately feared as some of the most powerful and nefarious wizards in all of Faerûn."

Szass Tam is a powerful necromancer. When he took over Thay, he turned its citizens into an undead legion loyal to him and his fellow necromancers. These undead cannot be killed by conventional means, which makes this danger brewing in Thay particularly scary. "It's a tricky concept to play someone who is essentially undead because it was interesting to try to understand if and how they emote," Head explains. "There's more dimension if it is rooted in something real and something emotional. So, I essentially didn't want her just to be bad for the sake of being bad. So, I developed my own very dark . . . back-story from when she was a child, and essentially, she felt she had nothing left to lose, which is why she decided to sacrifice her soul and become one of Szass Tam's undead. I think she emotes a lot of anger, as you'll see in the film. I think that the emotions of her past have kind of left a ghost of a blueprint on her soul that is no longer a soul."

Sofina hires Edgin and his band to break into a seemingly impenetrable stronghold to obtain an item from its vault. Sofina is the primary reason for Edgin and Holga's capture and imprisonment, as she and Forge double-cross the group. After this incident, Sofina works alongside Forge as his top adviser.

While Forge uses Sofina to aid his role as Lord of Neverwinter, she has her own nefarious reasons for teaming up with him. "Forge is essentially a pawn in the master plan," suggests Head. "Sofina basically has to do as Szass Tam says, and as much as she loathes Forge, she sees that it is the best opportunity to fulfill Szass Tam's goals."

Sofina is a *wizard*, a class of individuals that can wield magic after a period of intensive study. In DUNGEONS & DRAGONS, wizards are able to choose an *arcane tradition*—the study of a particular school of magic. Sofina is part of the School of Necromancy. Necromancy focuses on spells that control life and death, even allowing users of this magic school to animate the dead.

With Red Wizards being feared throughout the land outside of Thay, Sofina hides her true identity by wearing a cowl. This covers the arcane sigils permanently marked on the shaved heads of Red Wizards that visually identify their allegiance to Szass Tam. "The costume department has worked absolute miracles," confirms Head. "The details and just the use of the fabrics and the way that they've tailored it, and the cowl, and having the wire [in the robe's collar] that is able to shape it and mold it, it's just astonishing."

Magic isn't the only weapon that Sofina wields. She also carries a Red Wizard's blade, which brings swift death to anyone it cuts. "What we needed with Sofina was something that was a bit more vicious," Dunne explains. "That's also something that she hides under her cloak. So, you'll never see this on her person, as in, worn on the belt, or in a sheath. So, this is always held. This is always hidden under her sleeve, so you'll only see it when you need to."

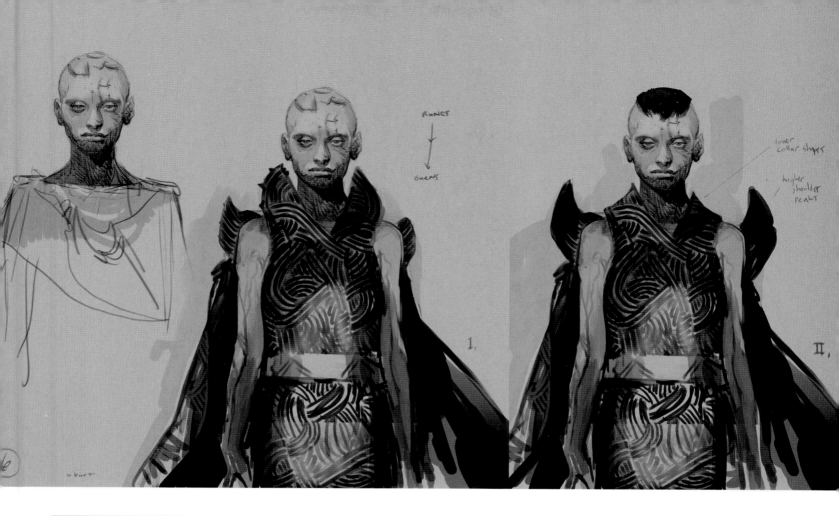

GORG

Two years into Edgin and Holga's sentence, another prisoner is added to their cell—Gorg, who is a hobgoblin, a type of humanoid that prides themselves on their physical strength. The film opens with Gorg being escorted through Revel's End Prison, and he is the first character introduced to audiences. "He basically is a mislead for our intro to the movie," Goldstein discloses. "We want the audience to think that they're watching a traditional Lord of the Rings–type of a scene, and then he's put in a cell with our heroes and they quickly dispatch him and we never see him again for the rest of the film."

"You kind of play like this is a very important character," Latcham states. "This guy's going to get his butt kicked by Michelle Rodriguez about five minutes into the film, and it's going to be a big surprise."

These tall and muscular creatures have a distinct look. The filmmakers relied on special makeup effects to transform actor Spencer Wilding into the creature. "He's seven foot tall," Wilding notes. "He's not a very nice man—or hobgoblin—and he's very nasty."

THE ABSOLUTION COUNCIL

The Absolution Council is in charge of governing Revel's End. They are a committee of various representatives from the Lords' Alliance, which is a confederation of rulers of cities and towns across Faerûn with a united goal of safety and prosperity for their lands. One of the Council's tasks is to conduct prisoner hearings, where inmates are brought forth and given the opportunity to plead their case for early release.

As Edgin and Holga were convicted of the same crime, they are given a shared hearing. It is during this time that Edgin regales the council with their story in a way that only a bard could.

There are four members of the film's Absolution Council: Chancellor Anderton, Baroness Torbo, Chancellor Jarnathan, and Chancellor Norixius.

Chancellor Anderton and Baroness Torbo

Chancellor Anderton is a human, which makes a great visual contrast when he's seated next to Baroness Torbo. Torbo is a halfling, a people who are similar to humans, but are about half as tall. "We have a full-size actress and we're scaling her down," VFX supervisor Ben Snow affirms of the actor who plays Baroness Torbo. "So, we built an enormous chair for her to sit in so she looks small in the chair, and then we have this giant chair on set with the other characters, and then that gets shrunk down in postproduction to make her [small]. So, she's 3'6" in the film from being 5'6" in real life."

Chancellor Jarnathan

Chancellor Jarnathan is an aarakocra, a birdlike humanoid creature that has both arms and fully functioning wings, and taloned feet. "[He] could have been a fully CG character, but we thought it would be really fun to try to make him a man in a costume with state-of-the-art animatronics and puppeteering," exclaims Daley.

It was important to both directors that Jarnathan look and feel authentic. Enter Legacy Effects—a special-effects company that specializes in prosthetics, animatronics,

and creature design. "One of the other characters that I really loved from the initial meetings and the read was Jarnathan," says Shane Mahan, one of the co-founders of Legacy Effects. "There was a lot of talk about, 'Can you guys pull this off? There's a lot of costume and animatronics, and the directors would really not like it to be fully CGI if you guys can do a character.' And I foolishly said, 'Yes, I think we can do it, because there are elements of things we've done—wings, animatronic heads, extended feet—it's all stuff that we've done before in some way or another.' But putting it all together as one was a fun challenge."

In the end, the wizards at Legacy Effects were able to pull it off. "The wings move, the eyes move—it's so realistic," Rodriguez notes of Jarnathan's final look. "It's just fantastic to have something to play off of that's not green screen. And it's really beautiful to see the talent that gets involved. They hand-paint this stuff. They mold it from scratch. I mean, I'm hanging out with the Legacy boys and they are my favorite people on set because these guys are so talented. They're sitting there painting on canvases and molding and shaping all of these creatures from scratch."

For the final build, Jarnathan's head is an animatronic mask. "The mouth needs to talk," Mahan explains. "It needs to blink and do various things, so we kind of mimic, as he's speaking, the mouth movement, there's tongue movement. . . . As the actor's talking, we can hear him through it and just follow along. There's not a sophisticated playback system or anything."

The attention to detail didn't end there. "The hands have articulated extension, so that when he moves his fingers, it actually creates these joints to move," says Mahan. "So, making a three-fingered bird hand was important to do. And same with the feet. Feet are like just stilt versions that you can wear, and they will support him up quite a few inches off the ground. It makes him even higher. So, he's walking on basically an articulated pair of high-heel shoes, right? And it really increases his height. And then, to add even more misery to him, we've got a set of articulated wings."

NORMAL/STOIC   WORRIED   PANICKED

Aarakocra V1

Jarnathan's Wings

Jarnathan's wings were a massive build. "They weigh probably sixty pounds," adds Mahan. "It's a backpack that goes on. It's a self-contained mechanism of wings that extended open ten or eleven feet out."

More than one costume for Jarnathan was made depending on the needs of what was being shot. "There'll be some times where he's not wearing the feet so he can be really grounded," Mahan explains. "There's a stunt version of this, too, because we've shot a lot of action scenes where it's flying on wires."

Chancellor Norixius

Another fantastical humanoid sits on the Absolution Council. Chancellor Norixius is a dragonborn, a species of creatures that look like dragons, but stand erect and walk on two legs. Dragonborn have colorful scales and the ability to cause destruction with their breath—such as fire, poison, or lightning—just like the much larger dragons of their ancestry. In traditional DUNGEONS & DRAGONS, dragonborn do not have tails or wings. "A dragonborn is a playable type in DUNGEONS & DRAGONS," mentions Jeremy Jarvis, senior creative director at Wizards Franchise Development. "They're one of the larger silhouettes and they have a fearsome appearance, but can be as benevolent as the player wants them to be."

To bring Norixius to life, the filmmakers once again turned to Legacy Effects. "He's a Legacy Effects practical makeup that a really good actor was wearing," says Snow. "Being able to talk—his face was manipulated by remote, sort of face-sensing software. So, someone was puppeteering him with their face at real time, all working. His lips are in sync with what the actor's doing."

"[What] an incredible experience just seeing the development of that character," exclaims Daley of Norixius. "They used face-capture technology to actually emulate facial expressions in a way that I had never seen before done in a movie this scale."

NORIXIUS

Dragonborn

Norixius isn't the only dragonborn in the film. Others populate the land—like a dragonborn beggar—to help flesh out the world. "One of the things we're always looking for is that beyond-human silhouette lineup," says Jarvis. "That is a big part of D&D as well, and again, further differentiates us from some other fantasy properties where the weirdest you get is a diminutive character, or pointed ears. Well, we have much more fantastical folk that populate the land, like tieflings, like dragonborn, so trying to make sure those show up to, again, build out that texture of what is wonderful about D&D."

Actors loved having these creatures created practically, and not relying on computer graphics to execute. "When you have amazing animatronic creatures to react to, it really does change your performance," notes Rodriguez. "It's a big difference between a golf ball and a dragonborn animatronic creature in front of you. This just makes night-and-day difference in the performance and in your experience making a movie. You just really feel the effort of people and it pushes you to be better."

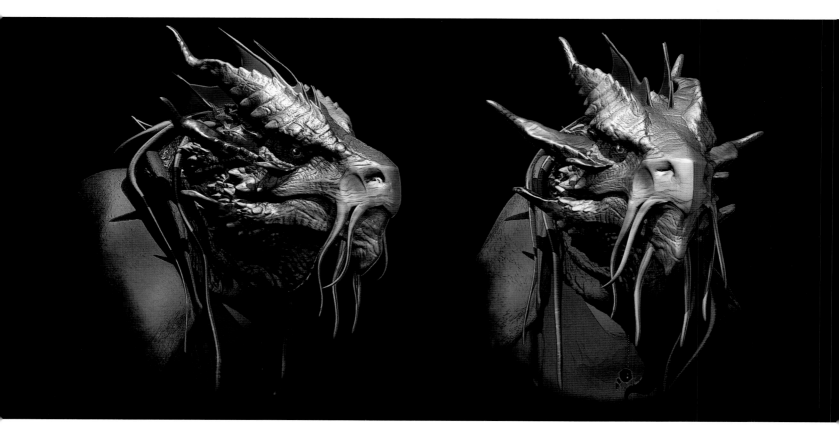

MARLAMIN

Holga's ex-husband Marlamin is a middle-aged halfling who loves to garden. "Holga has a storied history with him," observes Daley. "She left her tribe to be with him. Her tribe was very insular and didn't accept outsiders, and she took the ultimate sacrifice of leaving her family and her people to follow this romance, which ultimately fell apart because of her inability to let go of her, her family ties."

After breaking up with Holga, Marlamin has since remarried. His new wife, Gwinn, also happens to be a barbarian. Despite their relationship falling apart, Holga still thinks Marlamin is one of the finest men in Faerûn. When their travels bring them near Marlamin's cottage, Holga feels compelled to stop; they finally have a real conversation about what happened, and Holga gains some long-needed closure.

To sell the idea of a halfling's small stature, like Marlamin, several tricks are used. "We shot scale composites, but our halflings really are half human size," says Snow. "They're very, very small, and so it brings up a lot of challenges as to everyone's patience . . . because you've got to film the scene and then you've got to film the scene again sometimes with the camera or the subject farther away, and then, know that we're going to be able to blend those two in postproduction, so it takes time, but one of the things that John and Jonathan are really wanting to do is trying to do things for real as much as possible and have real backgrounds, real environments as much as we can."

In addition to camera work and visual effects, other techniques were used to fully realize the character's intended scale. "When designing Marlamin's costume, we had to consider how the full-size costume would be replicated in a child size for the body double," explains Monk. "Therefore, any trim and detail had to be scaled down, so it was important to keep the design simple so the smaller version would still look balanced."

XENK
YENDAR

DRALAS AND THE THAYAN ASSASSINS

When Edgin and Holga manage to escape from their planned execution, Sofina isn't worried at first. It isn't until they reemerge that the adventuring group's meddlesome nature begins to worry her. Sofina doesn't want anyone to interfere with Szass Tam's plans. Looking for someone to eliminate Edgin and his team, Sofina turns to a fellow countryman to track them down. "Dralas is a bit of a rock star," claims actor Jason Wong. "He is part of the undead team. . . . We are undead. You can't kill us. We'll always keep coming back."

Costumes visually help convey their undead nature. "We started with Dralas, working to create the aged, undead quality of him," explains Monk. "His costume was layered and distressed to give the impression of pieces acquired over time, and many battles won. We then designed the rest of the assassins around him, keeping to the dark, sinister color scheme, and aged fabrics to make them look like a recognizable fighting band of assassins. There was also the challenge of making them look threatening and armored, but also leaving enough skin exposed to show their Thayan markings and reveal their ability to heal when wounded."

When Dralas and his group of Thayan assassins catch up with Edgin and his team, they discover that master swordsman Xenk Yendar has joined the party. During the pursuit, Dralas wields an intricate sword that he uses in his battle with Xenk, who proves to be a formidable match. "He's one of these characters who doesn't die, so we've fairly given this [sword a] bit of a web feel to it," discloses Dunne. "He's got that [same pattern] within his costume." His sword comes with a special feature. "What we've tried to deal with is separation," Dunne continues. "You can see the double blades on this. So, the idea of this is it's been the sword catcher. So, within the fight area, he's able to catch a sword in between and lock it in. And so, I see it in one of his fights—we'll have that with Xenk, and you'll see a lot of work with that."

SZASS TAM

Head necromancer Szass Tam lurks in the shadows, commanding his legion of undead to execute his bidding. He used to be one of eight zulkirs who co-ruled Thay, but over a century earlier, he sought more power for himself and seized control using dark magic. Now Szass Tam is no longer satisfied ruling just Thay—he wants to take over all of Faerûn. "Szass Tam is trying to extend his power and his empire," states actor Ian Hanmore. "He uses people in that way, you know? He uses the undead, and he uses the living as lackeys. He, himself, can appear in different forms. Always, he's striving to increase his power."

Sofina is key in helping Szass Tam achieve his plans to overthrow the city of Neverwinter. "He's basically on a complete power trip and wants to expand the Thay empire and rule as much of Faerûn as he can," remarks Head. "And Sofina is a very loyal and willing ally and servant to achieving his goals of domination." But she isn't the only Red Wizard aiding Szass Tam's quest for dominance. Other undead necromancers assist in Thay's dark plans. "The Red Wizards of Thay are a corrupt group of sorcerers who seek to promote chaos and misery," Smith explains. "They are trying to basically create an army of undead slaves in order to cultivate ultimate power. Our group has to stop that from happening—reluctantly at first—because throughout the film, our group goes from being motivated by self-interest to seeing the importance of helping others."

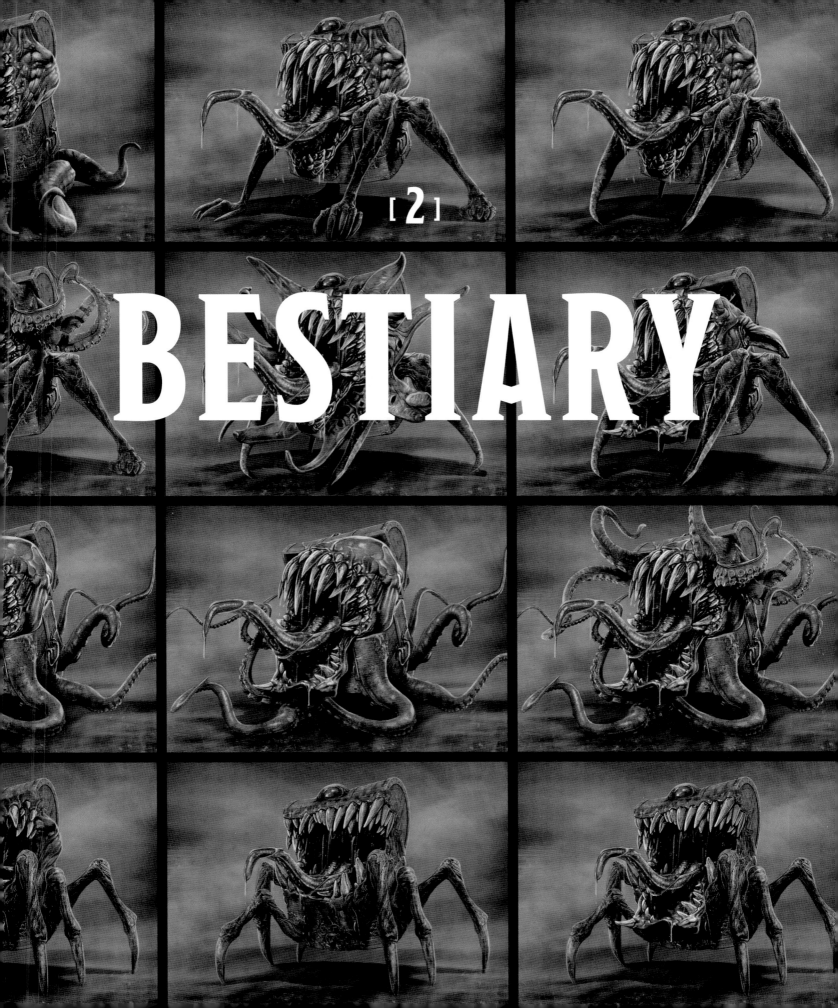

BESTIARY

[2]

CREATURES BOTH FRIENDLY & FIENDISH

THE WORLD IS A DANGEROUS PLACE. When you play a game of DUNGEONS & DRAGONS, there are a myriad of creatures you may encounter. From city streets to dense forests and swamps to deep underground caverns, beasts of all shapes and sizes lurk in every corner of Faerûn. DMs have hundreds of entities from which to choose, making sure every fraught encounter during a campaign is a surprise.

With so many monsters already established in D&D, there was no shortage of choices for the filmmakers to make their selection. "What we have that's great on this film is all the history of DUNGEONS & DRAGONS," says VFX producer Diana Giorgiutti. "And there's pages and pages and pages of incredible information. . . . And there will be the creatives, the powers that be, from the D&D world that will want us to adhere to all of that history and [pay] homage to the game, and all of the fans out there that know that sort of stuff, or that know that history, and that love the game. But then we want it to appeal to people that aren't as familiar. So I think part of the trick for us will be how to blend the two, how to keep that original lore true for all the big fans and the really serious fans, but at the same time cover the film fans and the story fans that'll be looking for something more realistic or more believable."

To create the creatures seen in the film, two different approaches were used. "It was important to us to find the right balance between practical effects and computer-generated ones," notes Goldstein. "We have two of the best [VFX] houses in the world—MPC [Motion Picture Company] and ILM [Industrial Light & Magic]—and they are doing incredible work in bring[ing] this world to life."

"[For practical effects,] we have the geniuses at Legacy Effects that have given you all of your favorite puppeteered characters—including Baby Yoda—basically helping to create some of these iconic characters and cultures from D&D," adds Daley. "We really tried to embrace the practical as much as we can. Like Jonathan said, finding that perfect balance between practical and CG that immerses audiences in a way that I think no one approach can."

The filmmakers also seized every chance they could to include creatures in unexpected ways. "What we started looking for were opportunities to ask, 'Hey—how do we make the presence of the breadth of monsters felt in the world without just adding more to the film and without extending the length [of the film]?'" reveals Jarvis. "There are creatures represented in mosaics, represented in artwork. So, you accomplish some of the world building for D&D through the in-world arts and crafts. Seeing them in sculptures, right? We were able to mount it on walls. We were able to get the presence felt without just adding more to an already very packed film."

SAPPHIRE DRAGONFLY

On the day that Edgin cremates his wife, Zia, he sees a sapphire dragonfly. This creature reappears at various points during the film, a constant reminder of the loss he suffered. "We wanted to have a sort of physical embodiment of the memory of Edgin's late wife, and we thought something natural, like a beautiful insect, would be kind of cool," recalls Goldstein. "We first see it at her funeral. It's sort of flying over her funeral pyre. And then later we get a glimpse of it there in a flashback that Edgin has where he's remembering a happy time with his wife. And then throughout the movie, we get glimpses of that dragonfly."

The sapphire dragonfly is the only creature in this bestiary that is not from the DUNGEONS & DRAGONS game.

Instead, it is a creation of both Goldstein and Daley—a narrative tool with a bigger meaning attached. "We wanted it to be ambiguous at first," adds Daley. "It's just that it's symbolism that Edgin associates with his wife. But then as you continue to watch the film and some context is provided, you realize that what it really symbolizes, beyond just the wife, is the idea of letting things go. Of being able to not try to capture a moment, to capture a time in your life when you were happy, because as we all know, life continues to move on and things evolve and people die and things change. And the only way to live with that is to embrace the next step."

AXE BEAK

Throughout the Triboar Plains, farmers tend to their axe beaks—large, flightless birds with a wedge-shaped beak that resembles an axe. At markets in the city of Neverwinter, they are often sold as food or transportation.

"There was an early design that was based on the classic DUNGEONS & DRAGONS axe beak, but the directors weren't super keen on it," recalls Snow. "Then, we found a bird—a shoebill. It's a very distinctive bird." Snow tasked Kevin Cahill, the second-unit VFX supervisor, with using Photoshop to add an axe beak's head onto a shoebill body to see if it had the right look. Snow continues, "He did a really good job of it. And we showed the directors and they're like, 'Yeah. That looks like the axe beak.' . . . In the end, they were so happy with this rough Photoshop job that it really became the creative on the way that the creatures would look."

RUST MONSTER

Be sure to protect your favorite blade, lest a rust monster come to corrode and devour it. These aptly named creatures feed on rust, and their touch breaks down any non-magical metal weapon nearby.

Although at one point these creatures were cut from the script, eventually the filmmakers were able to bring them back for a cameo, although not as the larger beasts first conceptualized. Snow explains, "The tricky part with that was taking the rust monsters, which are really big creatures, and making them feel like they were babies. We talked about maybe having an egg next to one like it had just broken out of the egg, but in the end, we just had the visual effects team try and give them baby things [features]. Like their eyes are a little bigger, and their limbs are smaller. And of course they're rust monsters, so they have to be fighting over a piece of metal."

DISPLACER BEAST

The displacer beast has the ability to displace light, making it seem as though it is not in its actual location. As creatures that like to stalk prey for both food and sport, these ferocious felines should be taken quite seriously. "To D&D fans, they may understand that a displacer beast can displace an image of itself in order to distract its prey, but it's such an unusual thing," explains Daley. "And the fact it has six legs, and the fact that it has these giant psionic paddles coming from its shoulders, you have to really help to explain the story of that to the people that don't know in a way that doesn't feel like a lesson."

"It was challenging because we have to educate the audience very quickly into how it works, and then pay it off," echoes Goldstein. "So that's why that poor little dwarf gets killed early on."

To figure out how to translate the displacer beast from paper onto film required the answering of several key questions. "We know the idea behind the displacer beast is it's not quite where you think it is, and so it's dangerous in several ways," says Jarvis. "How does that misdirection actually manifest on screen? What are you seeing? How is it hidden? How does it cloak itself? What does it project?"

Eventually the team figured out how to best show the displacer beast's duplication ability and movement.

"The creature looks like a panther, so we had some real-world reference of what it should generally look like," recalls Snow. "It has the paddles that come out that it actually uses to project a false image of itself. They were something that we had to evolve, but the design actually came together pretty well. The tricky part is it's got six legs and it's very difficult for the animators to get their heads around using those six legs. . . . One of these challenges was how do we make the animation exploit the fact that it's got six legs so it feels like it's justified. And that was a fair bit of work for the animation team."

The inclusion of the displacer beast was an easy decision for the directors. "We wanted it to bring out the things that make D&D special—the things that are very unique about it," adds Goldstein. "A lot of the creatures [are] in the sort of medieval fantasy world you've seen in other places, so we tried to do the ones that you haven't seen much of, and the displacer beast is a good example because it's so weird and specific and interesting."

OWLBEAR

Adventurers should proceed with caution when traveling in forests or caves—one creature you would not want to stumble upon there is an owlbear. If you do, watch out for its claws and beak. As half bear and half owl, they take traits from both animals. Although these beasts are unable to fly, their large size means that fighting one is no small feat.

The owlbear seen in the film is actually one of Doric's wild shapes. Because of that, several factors needed to be considered when coming up with the design. "With the early Doric owlbear, I was exploring what characteristics could carry over from her tiefling form, like her horns and jewelry," explains concept artist Tully Summers. "We were also searching for what kind of owl we wanted to base off, and just how monstrous and intimidating we wanted her to be. I started off with a great horned owl, and eventually landed on a snowy owl, which has a softer, more feminine feel to it, and the white feathers have a striking contrast."

"It's technically a monster in the world," claims Daley of the owlbear. "We didn't want it to be monstrous, and we always love the idea of one of our protagonists being that creature, and so we had to find a way in that was likable, aesthetically, with our owlbear. There's an inherent cuteness, too, to her, but there's also this predatory danger. So, it was finding that balance of keeping it imposing, but also pretty. You know, if you are prey, they are quite scary as well. So, it was kind of finding that balance of keeping it imposing and dangerous, but also pretty."

Owlbears are one of the most iconic beasts in DUNGEONS & DRAGONS, and it was a creature both filmmakers and Wizards of the Coast were excited to bring to the big screen. "The really fun part of adapting the owlbear, from my point of view, were the discussions about movement," Jarvis recalls. "Because it's unironically kind of a bear, and kind of an owl. So how much owl is in its movement? That was one of the things that we talked about. Of, like, 'Can we get that owl-like, really jerky head movement, while it is potentially lumbering in how it can move?' I remember the first time we saw the [VFX] turnaround of it trotting, for lack of a better term. The [filmmaking] team shared that with my [Wizards of the Coast] team, and there was literally applause in seeing that brought to life in its run cycle."

GIANT QUIPPER

In DUNGEONS & DRAGONS, quippers are carnivorous fish. More akin to piranhas in both size and shape for the game, the filmmakers decided to supersize this little fish for a key sequence in the film. "[When] we met Xenk Yendar, played by Regé-Jean Page, he was rescuing a baby tabaxi from [inside] an enormous fish," states Goldstein. "And because we chose to do those things practically, it was kind of amazing and surreal because we had an actual fifteen-foot fish."

To build the giant quipper, the filmmakers once again looked to Legacy Effects. "We were talking about the practical realities of that, and how much . . . we would have to rely on VFX [for this scene], but much to the credit of Legacy, they created this massive, flopping animatronic fish that's quite lifelike—and were able to create a wireless puppet of

this baby that wriggles around in an unsettlingly realistic way," recalls Daley. "We didn't think that every aspect of that could be done practically. We did some VFX work later to help add to the realism of it, but it was astonishing to us what they were able to do in such a short time frame, and I think it only adds to the immersive experience of the film."

The quipper was one of the more technical animatronics created. "All of the months and months that go into this work for the fish and this baby is about a minute and a half of screen time," comments Mahan. "But it doesn't matter because it's a great minute and a half. And hopefully it'll be one of those moments in the movie that really stands out, because we were very proud of it."

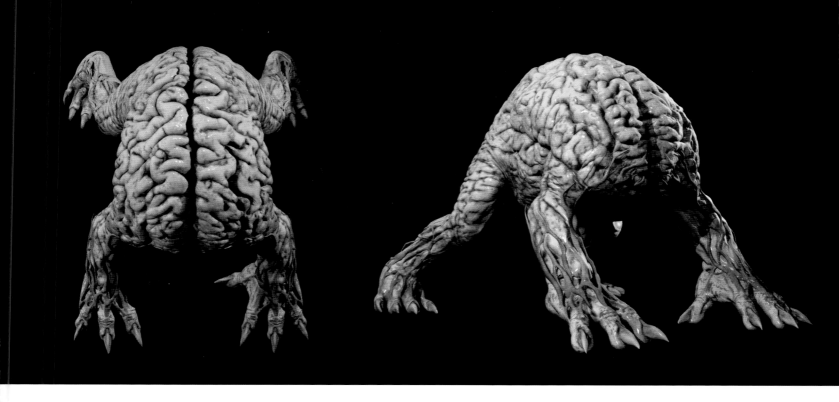

INTELLECT DEVOURER

Strange creatures live deep beneath the world's surface in the Underdark, perhaps none more bizarre than the intellect devourer. With a body shaped like a brain, the creature stalks on four clawed legs, searching for intelligent beings to consume—feeding on the target's mind, and taking control of their body. "We originally had conceived there being people inside these suits," recalls Snow of the intellect devourers. "Legacy Effects—who did all the practical creatures on the film and did a fantastic job of designing suits that we could put a person in, but in the end, the directors felt it made them too big—they wanted them to be the size of a medium-sized dog. It [also] meant they didn't quite have the freedom and agility that they could have if they were as computer graphics, so we ended up doing that instead."

"The intellect devourers went through a fun progression," recalls co–VFX producer Tyler Cordova. "The VFX on-set production team carried long painter's poles with orange tennis balls stuck onto the end of the poles to serve as eye-lines for the actors so they knew the timing of the creature's movement. We went from little orange tennis balls to slimy brain creatures with legs and claws. These creatures, to me, were a lot of fun to watch the progression on the animation and the renders—having these walking brains look and feel like living, breathing creatures, but also making sure they felt creepy and weird. Michael Langford, the animation supervisor at MPC, and his team did a fantastic job animating these creatures in a way that gave these little brains with legs personality."

Luckily for Edgin and his team, they spot a group of intellect devourers, but are able to remain hidden from the creatures. "The comedy in that moment when they [the intellect devourers] just walk on by our heroes, it's an insult that they didn't even bother to sniff them out—meaning they don't have any intelligence," laughs Giorgiutti. "So Edgin has a nice quip at the end of that one."

MIMIC CHEST

Adventurers should be wary during a campaign, for not all objects may be as they appear. A shapeshifting beast known as a mimic might be hiding in plain sight, trying to lure unsuspecting adventurers close so it can attack. These creatures are able to shift their appearance to resemble basic materials, and can take the form of useful objects, like a door or a book. However, no mimic shape is more iconic than that of a chest. "The mimic is definitely one of our more ownable creatures," notes Jarvis. "The concept of something masquerading as something inanimate when it is, in fact, animate . . . and they can masquerade as things other than chests—but that chest with the teeth, with the maul, with the tongue, is something we were very glad to see in the film."

"Our overall VFX Supervisor, Ben Snow, and the team at ILM had a daunting task to bring one of the most famous fantasy shapeshifting creatures to life,"

says Cordova. "The familiarity with the mimic outside of D&D created a high expectation to get it right, so when it shows up on the big screen, fans of D&D and non-D&D alike can cheer together. The benefit of the mimic—particularly the mimic chest—being a familiar creature is the amount of reference that exists and is available to pull from, though many depictions of the mimic monster from video games and D&D lore were very hard to make photoreal. John and Jonathan had always had a clear idea of how the mimic chest should look: rows of retractable teeth, an absurdly long tongue, like the chest itself is a living creature, unlike its depictions in other lore where it sometimes sprouts legs and arms and grows a body. The end result is one of my all-time favorite creatures, which still makes me cheer even after having seen it so many times during all of our reviews."

GELATINOUS CUBE

The concept of a giant gelatinous cube might seem ridiculous at first, but don't be fooled. This slow-moving square of goop is deadly. Its large, translucent form makes it difficult to see—meaning unsuspecting adventurers may walk directly into its body and become stuck. If you get caught by this creature and are not able to wriggle free, be prepared to slowly dissolve until there is nothing left but your bones inside the armor that couldn't protect you. "I think the challenge with the gelatinous cube is really the physics of it," explains Jarvis of bringing the gelatinous cube to the big screen. "Like, once you do interact with it, once you are stuck in it, how does that actually affect you? How much can you move? How quickly? What is the amount of resistance as you encounter it? And so, the gelatinous cube is a really fun concept. It's basically a big slab of dangerous Jell-O that moves very slowly, and unless you're really paying attention, you can just not see the thing because of its translucency. Grounding that [concept] in the film reality, I think, was probably the challenge there. Of something that could be very, very silly, but needs to actually be pretty dangerous, and making it a part of a world with physics."

The filmmakers relied on the special-effects team to come up with creative ways to show actors interacting with the cube practically. "The gelatinous cube sequence, it's tricky 'cause, obviously, it's a solid in a kind of liquid form," says SFX supervisor Sam Conway. "Every time someone goes and puts their hand in it, or their body goes into it, it has to [be] absorbed into it without pushing it aside. So that was a very tricky one for research and development but it's in all sorts of different types of materials— silicone, waxes, liquids, gels, all that sort of stuff—and we discovered there was quite a good interaction with some of the waxes that we were using. . . . We [also] used the thin silicone sheets that have that kind of impact, so the resistance of impact."

Filming the sequence with the cube had its own set of challenges. The actors needed to ensure there would be continuity as they moved from shot to shot, pretending to be stuck inside. "The gelatinous cube was really cool," recalls Smith. "I'm covered in some sort of gel material. That was cool. And also having to freeze position. What sucked is if you froze in one position in one setup, you had to commit to that position every setup."

MORE CREATURES
FROM THE WORLD OF D&D

From animated armor to zombies, hundreds of creatures exist within in the world of DUNGEONS & DRAGONS. With so many options, it was obvious to the filmmakers that not every monster would make the cut, and deciding which beasts to include was a daunting task. "There's a ponderous amount of content, so a lot of our thinking is about cooking it down to what we want the audience to know," Jarvis explains. "What creatures are most ownable? What do we want the filmgoers to know about our dragons? Which classes do we want to make sure are represented so we can start to build that awareness with new viewers? Because the existing fans know that. They already have their favorite class. They have their favorite creatures. They have the creatures they never want to encounter. And so, we're looking to build that connective tissue for the wider audience. Those are the things we're constantly trying to push to see represented."

One of the most famous creatures that didn't make the cut was a beholder—a large, multi-eyed sphere that can fly and is capable of magic. With eyes in all directions, sneaking up on one of these monstrosities is all but impossible. "The beholder is a really good example of something that didn't make it," recalls Jarvis. "We would love to see a beholder done justice on the big screen, and we eventually will."

Beholder

Gray Render

Carrion Crawler

Ettin

Dretch

Troglodyte

DRAGONS

ADVENTURERS BEWARE. One of the largest and most fearsome beasts that you can come across in the game is a dragon. The titular creature comes in many forms, each with different types of powers. "There are differences between DUNGEONS & DRAGONS dragons, and a lot of what you see in other properties," explains Jarvis. "There are, so far as evil dragons go, five main chromatic dragons—red, black, blue, white, green—and they all have different breath weapons. So, not every dragon in DUNGEONS & DRAGONS breathes fire. So, we definitely wanted to see some of that differentiation brought to the screen because it's a thing that we enjoy about D&D a lot."

In DUNGEONS & DRAGONS, chromatic dragons are evil. Black dragons breathe out acid. Blue dragons can breathe out lightning. Green dragons breathe out poisonous gas. White dragons exhale ice or frost. Red dragons, the most powerful of all, breathe out fire. Not all dragons in the game have malicious intent, however. Metallic dragons—like bronze, copper, gold, and silver—are generally good. Although these dragon types have famously helped adventuring parties, even these beasts have been known to attack when provoked.

RAKOR (BLACK DRAGON)

The first dragon that the audience sees in the film is Rakor, a black dragon. Rakor is in a flashback during a great battle. Blasting down soldiers with his acid breath, the beast is nothing short of terrifying. "The dragon is always, for us, it's always a big thing to put into the mix," states Conway. "With our previous jobs, we've done plenty of fire and dragons, and this time around, it changed to acid impacts rather than fire. . . . We had to really think quickly about how we do this. And we referenced lots of videos of research into acid—strong acids and how they affect metal, meats, and stuff like that. So, that was our approach for that. And we applied ourselves in kind of the acid form of smoke and dissolving-type effects. But then, of course, you'll have to do that on the [battle]field, so you are going to go bigger and apply it to costumes, to the floor, and stuff."

"Sam Conway in special effects came up with something where he basically splattered these guys with goo that had smoke emitters on their backs, so it looked like it was acid burning," recalls

Snow. "[When filming,] your hope is you work out what the effect is going to look like before you shoot, because then you can say, 'Hey Sam. Give me some white smoke on the ground as if the acid's burnt the ground,' and he'll do that. When you've got this many effects, its rarely possible to do all of that ahead of time, but with the acid it was a really good thing."

Rakor is very typical of what one might expect when imagining a dragon. "We wanted to find a way to add a more traditional DUNGEONS & DRAGONS dragon, even if it was relatively brief," explains Jarvis. "And that is a lot of Rakor's role, the black dragon, in the film. By seeing this standard dragon, that kind of sets our expectations of what a dragon is—and then we see Themberchaud, and we're like, 'Oh wow! I was not expecting that.'"

THEMBERCHAUD (RED DRAGON)

Themberchaud, the red dragon, is not your traditional dragon. Quite simply, he's very well fed. "Themberchaud was always in the script from the first time I saw it," recalls Jarvis. "And Themberchaud is not representative of a standard D&D red dragon, right? He's a big boy, and has a different silhouette. The intention is that you deliver the expected in an unexpected way, and so we're introduced to this dragon that is very dangerous, but also is very large and pretty round."

Don't let his size fool you. Themberchaud is just as deadly. "Themberchaud is a dragon that, actually, it has probably feasted on a few too many adventurers and gotten pretty big," VFX supervisor Ben Snow notes. "So, he's still scary and threatening. He'd still eat you in a heartbeat, and there's still a lot of thread that we have to make real in the sequence. So, the actors are still having to [perform, like], 'Are we going to get eaten?' And they're being chased, and they're running for their lives, but at the same time, they can't help—particularly a character like Edgin—can't help but notice and comment that this dragon has eaten a few too many adventurers."

"We're not taking away the stakes of this guy," states Goldstein. "Themberchaud is a terrifying, man-eating monster—and he does eat several people in the sequence. So, they laugh, and then they realize, 'Oh. He's not that funny. . . .' They die if they fall into his clutches."

"It's a testament to John and Jonathan's sensibility," Snow says of Themberchaud's design. "It's DUNGEONS & DRAGONS. You have to have dragons, and the dragons have to look believable and good and hold up—but of course they're like, 'Yeah, but how do we change this so it's not expected?'"

To bring Themberchaud to life, filmmakers looked at references of creatures found on Earth. "With the dragon, we studied things like predatory [animals]," explains Snow. "For the animation of the dragon, what we're looking at as we get into actually animating him, as we're starting into postproduction, is we looked at real alligators running, and then we looked at obese alligators. But we also looked at obese dogs, and seals flopping around, and things that are little bit more humorous to look at. So, we're trying to get a nice blend. . . . As far as the actors were concerned, they would make wry comments about him, but we really wanted them to be focused on the threat of the dragon and making him look real."

FORGOTTEN REALMS

FAERÛN

WITH YOUR CHARACTER CREATED, adventuring party formed, and a basic knowledge of the various beasts you might encounter, you may wonder where your adventures will take place. While DMs are able to construct a fantasy setting of their own from scratch, many will choose to set the campaign in a world already created by Wizards of the Coast. One of the most popular settings from which DMs can choose is called the Forgotten Realms. "We knew we had to do the franchise and the fans justice," says Daley. "And one way to do that was to focus on one particular area, and not have to explore every facet of the game and the world because it is limitless almost. So, we take place in the Forgotten Realms, and basically focus on what's taking place in the Sword Coast with our crew of characters."

The Sword Coast is part of the northwest continent of Faerûn. This region sits alongside the Sea of Swords, and has vast tracts of untamed wilderness—from dense forests and rolling hills to snowcapped mountaintops and a frozen tundra. Some people have homesteads in the wilderness, while others live in villages or in cities. To choose the Sword Coast locations in which the story takes place took careful planning. "[We] were making sure that it was actually travelable," explains Jarvis. "They can't just teleport around. So, we said, 'Hey. From this place, what is the blast radius of where the story can take place?' We were making sure that people that are really, really in the know that would be watching and would recognize the places, would not be, like, 'Hey. I'm now taken out of this movie. This is no longer authentic.'"

Once the filmmakers decided where in Faerûn the story would be set, they worked on creating an authentic and fun visual world. The requirements from the directors were simple. "They just wanted the design of the movie to have, obviously, a sense of history, visual aesthetic, and not [be] too dour," says production designer Raymond Chan. "When I say *dour*, a lot of medieval films are very, very boring with a similar palette—very brown, very somber.

So, the one thing they made me cognizant of is, just give it a little bit more color and texture."

Other than those basic requests, the art department was free to create concepts at will. "John and Jonathan—they just had literally given me free rein," observes Chan. "There's obviously a classical way to re-create a fantasy film or medieval film, and they just said, 'Ray, we'd just like to see something unique. It's a brilliant platform, the new DUNGEONS & DRAGONS, and just have some fun with it.'"

Soon enough, Chan and his team were pumping out elaborate sets—either built on soundstages, or constructed at various locations, most of which were in Northern Ireland. "Ray Chan, our production designer on the film, is one of the best designers working in Hollywood," says Latcham. "I had worked with him as a supervising art director on *Avengers: Age of Ultron* and *Guardians of the Galaxy* and knew he was the right designer to bring the world of DUNGEONS & DRAGONS to life. I am so happy with how he was able to translate the rich world of the books into a fully realized cinematic world."

"What a special, special talent," echoes executive producer Denis L. Stewart about Chan. "He's the Energizer Bunny. He's just an amazing visionary and talent. I'd hire Ray Chan again and again and again and again. He's just awesome."

"I think one of the main highlights was showing up to the set each day to find a whole new world has been built by our incredible production designer Ray Chan, who really took it upon himself to make this thing look different from any other fantasy film that had ever been portrayed before," exclaims Goldstein. "There's so much diversity in each location and set that it was like Christmas morning every time we showed up on set to see what we had in store for us."

ICEWIND DALE

The film opens in Icewind Dale, a frozen tundra in the northernmost part of Faerûn. "Icewind Dale is a snowy ice landscape, very cold, very harsh," explains Conway. "So, we had to kind of think along those lines. We made what appeared to be collectively a concrete car park [into something] that looked like an ice sheet. And we spent a lot of time experimenting with resins and stuff like that to give us that look. . . . Bubbles trapped in the ice and all that sort of thing. So, we did certain patches of that to help kind of sell that. And, also, all the snow dressing as well. . . . Just a blizzard look—fans and foams."

Viewers will immediately understand the remote desolation of Icewind Dale from the opening shot of a horse-drawn transport carriage moving across a frozen river. "Sam Conway's special-effects team was able to rig up a practical coach so that it felt like we had a coach that we could shoot here on an artificial snow thing that they laid down," says Snow. "It's a sled but it's actually on wheels." While the icy ground and carriage were created practically, the filmmakers would need to rely on visual effects to complete the shot. Plates—a photographic layer that can be merged, or composited, with the primary camera footage to create a final scene—were taken to help sell the scene. "We originally were planning to shoot the scenes in Iceland, but with COVID, with the pandemic, it was impossible to take everything we needed through to Iceland at the time," recalls Snow. "We were able to send a crew over to take a bunch of plates and found some terrific locations there that we could shoot a lot of really cool backgrounds. . . . We had to sort of innovate and ended up shooting bluescreen on that and then tying that into these backgrounds that we shot previously in Iceland."

"We shot aerial plates from a helicopter when we needed to be high off the ground, like wide shots when Edgin and Holga escape ," explains Cordova. "We also shot a ton of footage ground level off of a specially rigged snowmobile for the carriage entrance, and off of a tripod in an Icelandic valley in the middle of nowhere for the ice chopping scene. . . . We were also very fortunate to witness the eruption of an active volcano while we were shooting plates in Iceland. The shot of Edgin and Holga riding past an erupting volcano was real, and shot off a helicopter in Iceland—my all-time favorite plate ever."

Towering above the icy ground is Revel's End, a remote prison that receives the nastiest of Faerûn's criminals. The prison's exterior gate was constructed for filming. "This was a practical build on the backlot where we build the exterior façade of Revel's End," says Chan. "The chain mechanism was engineered on a separate rig, so we actually pushed the entire carriage into the doorway almost like an airlock. So basically, the prisoner could never escape."

While Revel's End is now part of DUNGEONS & DRAGONS canon, it wasn't when the filmmakers first began working on the film. "One of the coolest parts of this process was we created this—this prison in Icewind Dale," exclaims Goldstein. "That didn't exist in the lore. And we spoke to the Wizards [of the Coast team] about it and they included that in the game. So now if you play [*Icewind Dale:*] *Rime of the Frostmaiden*, you see that piece of the movie in the game. And in many ways, that's this great sort of symbiosis between the two entities."

Inside Revel's End, individual cells wrap around a central watchtower. This type of prison design is called a panopticon. "It's a Victorian prison structure," explains Snow. "Basically, you would make the prison so that you could easily supervise people because it's a big cylinder. So, from the middle you can sort of see all the cells around the edge, and vice versa. The film tries to set it up."

The stonework inside and around the cells was cleverly constructed. "We bought hewn slate slabs, which we smashed, and then made molds," says Chan. "That created the entire wall surface. So, it's not something that we sculpted. It's something that we bought from a quarry, and then just re-created all the walls, the ceilings, and indeed the floor." Covering various surfaces inside the prison is a viscous substance that the art department created and ended up calling *dragon grease*. "We came up with a wallpaper paste, which we tinted with green pigment, and that was our dragon grease born," Chan continues.

Not everywhere in Revel's End is gloomy and covered in dragon grease. Within the tower is the Council Chamber, where prisoners go to petition the Absolution Council for release.

KORINN'S KEEP

Sitting atop a sea stack, Korinn's Keep is a seemingly impenetrable stronghold in the Korinn Archipelago, an island chain in the Sea of Swords. "Korinn's Keep is, in fact, a natural formation," observes Chan. "There's many around the world. This one was based in Donegal [Ireland], what we call a sea stack. The idea of the set is, primarily, it's two hundred feet tall, twenty stories tall, and the guys have hewn all the way down to almost sea level."

Within the keep's walls is a vault filled with priceless artifacts. Edgin and his band of thieves attempt to break into this vault—with disastrous results. "The alarm system is something that is triggered," Chan continues. "[It's] like a normal burglar alarm, but rather [than] just an alarm siren or a flashing light, we thought it would be really cool to have a stream of flame, which basically ignites fuel and traces all the way around the set in a split second."

Although Edgin and Holga are arrested during this heist, and later sent to Revel's End, Sofina gets the object she desires from the fortress to carry out Szass Tam's scheme—a horn that is key to performing a deadly spell that can quickly turn masses of people into the undead. "Korinn's Keep is where the horn is," says Head. "So, once she can get her hands on that, that is then the impetus, the starting point, for the *beckoning death* [spell] and ultimately achieving the climax, and achieving Szass Tam's intentions."

"Essentially, it is the thing that enables the spell to work," explains Latcham of the horn. "You need it to pass the [spell's] red mist to the large crowd that has been assembled. It is like a conduit that pulls the tendrils down and then blasts them out to the people in the form of a gaseous horror."

TARGOS

Edgin is from Targos, a fishing village on the edge of Icewind Dale. "[It] is where Edgin and Zia live with their daughter, Kira," says Chan. "We visit his town several times, not only in flashback, but also once Holga and Edgin have escaped Revel's End. In the lore, it's a very cold place right by a lake, so I took inspiration from this community in northern Japan where a lot of the thatched roofs would be so steep they would never hold any snow, and so basically that was the main inspiration. Not only that, they were self-insulating, so they were literally two feet deep [of] compacted thatch, which we don't normally see in England or anywhere else in the world. . . . Even the walls themselves, we just made little bundles of straws, so it all feels like a quilt-y jacket."

The construction of Targos's buildings was given interesting elements. "The windows are very delicate, where we broadened the casement window, or sash window," explains Chan. "The opening pane is on a pin and pivots ever so slightly. [It's] just having fun with different architectural details. The walls themselves are a riff on wattle and daub, which is historically used on any medieval film, it's essentially twigs and clay."

Targos was the first area in which filmmakers were able to add bright colors to the world. "We used French enamel varnish on the straw on the roofs, and it just gives it a more supple [look] and more like the straw itself was still alive and not completely dead. . . . We [also] brought in, I think about ten, fifteen tons of bedrock, which we sank into the ground and we dressed with beautiful little Swiss alpine flowers and ground-covering hardy plants that you'd find that would only survive in cold climates, like juniper," Chan continues.

The town of Targos was constructed from scratch. "This is a farm here in Northern Ireland called [the]

Clandeboye Estate," says Latcham. "It's a big piece of farm property, and we came in, built this entire village right here on the farm, and put in this whole set—interior, exterior sets. . . . The outdoors gets us out of the studio, off the stage, and able to live in the environment. It gives a little bit more of a real patina to it. It's really nice. And Ray Chan . . . just did a great job of taking this piece of land and making it become this village that I've never quite seen before. We had to bring in special thatchers to do these roofs. It's like a really fine art of roof patching that's apparently a bit of a lost art, and I think Ray has done an incredible job of bringing that to life. And overall, the place just has this like incredibly vibrant feel to it."

The vibrant colors introduced in Targos carried over into Edgin and Zia's home. "[Fantasy films] tend to revert back to brown—brown timbers and brown furniture and brown floor—where I'm trying to introduce more color into this," Chan reveals. "So, in fact, a lot of the timbers have been sealed with a blue, blue-black wax, which is almost a preservative in this cold climate. So, you'll see a lot more color."

The colors of Targos change over time. "Earlier in the movie, in the flashbacks, we see kind of an idyllic version of Targos," Latcham continues. "It's beautiful. You kind of have these memories of Ed[gin] in his life with Zia, and everything was really great. . . . And when he comes back, it is now cold and gray and overcast, and we kind of understand it. It has a little bit of a journey to go on as a character to get back to a better life. So, this snow is there to kind of remind us of the journey that Ed[gin]'s going to go on over the course of the film."

Color was a key design element for filmmakers not just in Targos, but throughout Faerûn. "We've kept things a little brighter—a little lighter," says director of photography Barry Peterson. "Obviously there's very scary moments, and there's things that happen in this movie that play into the dark side, but we didn't go monochromatic partially in the production design. . . . We've stepped into a more colorful visual world."

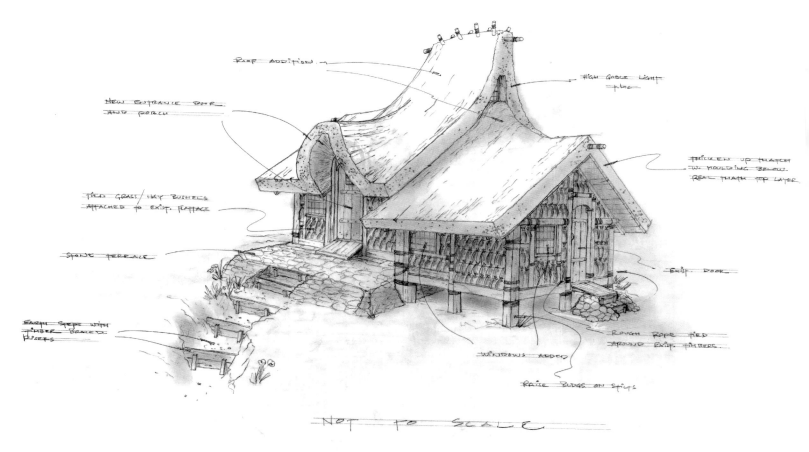

ROOF ADDITION

HIGH GABLE LIGHT
TUBE

NEW ENTRANCE DOOR
AND PORCH

THICKEN UP THATCH
W. MOULDING BELOW
REAL THATCH TOP LAYER

TIED GRASS/HAY BUSHELS
ATTACHED TO EXIST. FLATFACE

STONE TERRACE

EXIST. DOOR

EARTH STEPS WITH
TIMBER BRACED
RISERS

ROUGH ROPE TIED
AROUND EXIST. TIMBERS

WINDOWS ADDED

RAISE BLDGS ON STILTS

NOT TO SCALE

Trip and Shuffle Tavern

"The main tavern itself is called the Trip and Shuffle, which is where all the locals go for a pint of cider," states Chan of Targos's primary alehouse. "You can see even the floor itself is all what we called beam ends. I took inspiration from a Ford factory in Detroit . . . and gave that the signature [look] for the Trip and Shuffle."

Adorning the tavern's internal structure is a treasure trove of artifacts. "We worked very closely with the Wizards of the Coast on the project, so whenever [we had] the opportunity to incorporate some fan favorites from the realm into the environment, we would usually consult them for inspiration," says Moore. "With the Trip and Shuffle Tavern, I thought it would be really fun to have the features that you might find in a traditional tavern—like mounted heads—but with a D&D twist, so that it might take a second glance to notice that they are recognizable creatures. Things like the peryton worked perfectly

because they look like the deer heads you might find in a traditional old British tavern, but are a lot more magical. The hook horror claws look almost like antlers and were the perfect shape to frame the fireplace. We also made an illithid [mind flayer] tadpole in a jar which is tucked away on the bar as a little nod to *Baldur's Gate III.*"

Even the dishware contains hidden imagery if you know what to look for. "The cups being used by the background actors were made to look like they were made from Targos's famous scrimshaw, with knucklehead fish designs carved into them," adds Moore.

NEVERWINTER

Riding south from Targos along the coastal high road takes you to Neverwinter, one of Faerûn's cultural epicenters. "It's also called the Jewel of the North," says Chan. "It's a very historic city. It's cosmopolitan. It's very cultured. It's very bustling, like any city—New York, Sydney, London, Paris." As the name implies, it never gets cold. Although constructed in the north, Neverwinter sits on a river that is heated by a volcano, mysteriously kept warm by fire elementals. All adjacent areas never freeze over. The warm water is transported around the city via aqueducts. "The water sits at a regulated temperature," explains Chan. "So, they basically can irrigate their plants, their trees, all year long. And so, in order to convey that story, I thought to introduce some aqueducts—a way of carrying water irrigating the city, and also carrying water to the main castle."

Those waterways help maintain the city's green spaces. "My main inspiration is just taking a deep dive into the lore," Chan continues. "It's famed for its artisan craftsmen, and it's famed for its gardens. They have exquisite gardens here. So, my main inspiration for this was the Alhambra in Spain. It's very tropical. It's very Mediterranean—very dry, and very colorful, and very historical."

For filming, the entire city of Neverwinter was built from the ground up. "It is the single, most biggest build in the film," Chan divulges. "It's the longest in terms of the build time, and also the preparation, the set dressing involved. . . . Everything is bespoke, whether it be a table or stool. We're just trying to give it its uniqueness." Every nook and cranny was meticulously crafted. "The detail work is extraordinary," exclaims Pine. "It's a huge backlot. And the details in all of the crevices—I mean, the painting of these dragons on the walls, the things that aren't ever featured for their own sake, but add to the tapestry of the thing. And I guess it's really the job of working on these big films, is you get people at their absolute best. You get the best painters. You get the best construction people. You get the best production design, the best prop makers.

You get everybody [that] is the best of the best of the best of the best. So, walking onto Ray's sets is really just extraordinary. I think he's done something that obviously hearkens to ideas, images, and themes that we know, but he's done it in his own way."

"When planning the look for the Neverwinter streets, myself and Ray were really keen to stay away from the usual look of a medieval marketplace—with trestle-top brown wooden stalls selling bread and vegetables—so we took inspiration both from what we knew of the lore," adds Moore. "For example, that Neverwinter is famed for its lush gardens and craftwork, but also from D&D gameplay itself, incorporating stalls that sold rope, armor, tools, alchemy, [and] camping gear."

Dozens of extras were brought in for filming to help populate the city. "The street was just full of people in the clothing of the period, and goats and horses and weird-looking dogs, and the whole set was just decorated," recalls Smith. "It felt like we were transported back to that time, or that dimension, where all these fantastic elements exist." Colorful banners line the city streets. The blue-and-white ones bear the emblem of Neverwinter—three white snowflakes each enclosed in its own circle and arranged in a falling pattern. The gold-and-red ones announce a special event. "The gold-and-red banners, that's advertising the High Sun Games," states Chan.

In addition to simple banners, a special set was also created to hang above the main high street. "It's a really fun one . . . where as you progress toward the main square, the banners themselves are telling you the time of day," explains Chan. "So you'll see the flag, the sun itself is rising from nine o'clock, the next one will be ten o'clock, eleven o'clock, high noon, and it will drop down to sunset, so that's kind of a fun thing for the fans."

BREMEN

LONELYWOOD

TERMALAINE

CAER-DINEVAL

TARGOS

BRYN SHANDER

Hosted By The Lord of Neverwinter · Might Forge Fitzwilliam!

the **High** Glory Riches **Sun** Games

The World-Famous High Sun Games · Renowned Champions! · Magnificent Purse For The Victor!

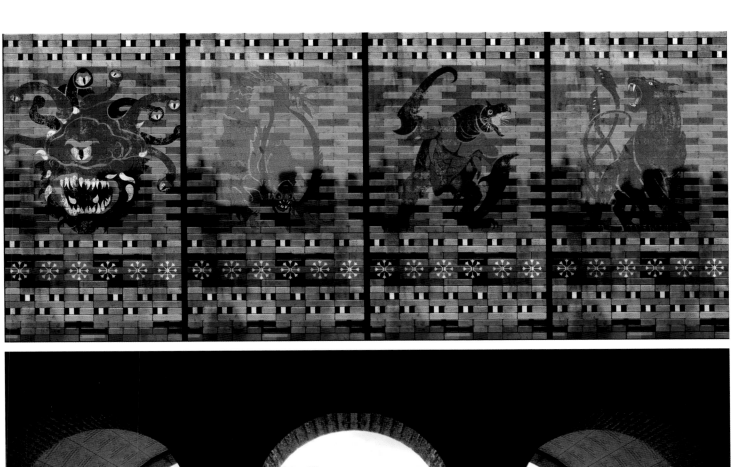

Castle Never

Castle Never is Neverwinter's main stronghold. It is here where Forge rules the surrounding lands as Lord of Neverwinter. "When our heroes get out of jail, they show up at Neverwinter and they're, like, 'Wait, the con man that we used to work with, that we used to pull jobs with, is now in charge of the entire city,'" says Latcham. "And that is not good for our heroes, because he has a lot of power. He has a lot of sway. And he can make their life very difficult."

While the exteriors of Neverwinter were fully constructed buildings and façades, many of Castle Never's interiors were shot at Wells Cathedral. Located in Somerset, England, construction on the church began late in the twelfth century, and it is the first English cathedral to be built in the Gothic style of architecture. "There's a certain amount of freedom given to us in interpreting the lore of DUNGEONS & DRAGONS, and one of those things that we had to interpret was what does Castle Never look like inside," Goldstein recalls. "And Wells Cathedral has this sort of regal beauty and timelessness, and it felt just right."

"It's this beautiful place—arch ceilings, these big, cavernous spaces, lots of cloisters, and it's just a beautiful, beautiful building," states Latcham. "The detail work here is fantastic. Our team has done a great job of trying to remove everything modern that's been put to the space and kind of restore it to its original glory. . . . We've also added some D&D touches. You'll see some beautiful busts of dragonborns, and of all kinds of beautiful things that

the art department has sculpted by hand to fill the place out, and we've added some beautiful tapestries. And, of course, the Neverwinter guards are in full effect in all their armor, and it's like a very regal place."

While most of the castle's interiors were shot inside Wells Cathedral, Forge's office was built on a soundstage. And it includes several unique elements, such as three reliefs on the back wall that tell the origin of Neverwinter. "I've taken inspiration from many, many different medieval castles and cathedrals out there," explains Chan of the office's design. "Forge's office is primarily based on parts of southern France—Rocamadour, Beynac, Sarlat—but the palettes themselves were something that I really wanted to get in. Rather than just have a painted mural, I thought we'd have a dimensional sculpt instead—the one that we first embarked on was the moment where Lord Never would be having a parley with the orc. It's almost like this is the final truth. 'Are you going to back off, or we're going to have a big-ass battle there?' So, that was my very first inspiration. The second one was the fact that the battle does happen and all the odds are against Lord Never because he's an elf and you've got all those nasty orcs. And the final sculpt was when Lord Never has actually destroyed the orc army. And the array of elves represent its coliseum, which is the birth of the arena. . . . I just wanted to give that to the fans, basically, the birthplace of Neverwinter, and I think it's just a subtle thing, you know?"

TRIBOAR PLAYHOUSE

Edgin and Holga are in need of a sorcerer, so they head to the crossroads town of Triboar, believing Simon will be there. Once they arrive, they find a small playhouse where Simon performs magic for a small crowd. "The idea behind the playhouse is that it was an essential space where people who are passing through can stop in for a bit of theater or entertainment," says art director Erin E. Riegel. "And that is where we find Simon doing his best to entertain—or, rather, rob—the masses."

The apron on the bottom of the stage is decorated in a specific motif. "This mural is meant to depict the story of the origin of Triboar, as well as what it means today," Riegel continues. "Triboar's name is thought to reflect the tale of the traveler, who, while coming through, was able to kill three boars on the same day. Outside of Triboar is also the resting place of Gwaeron Windstrom, and he is the god of rangers. So, rangers and travelers come through, traveling a great distance to pay tribute to Windstrom in hopes of having a good hunt when they do their ranger thing."

The stage's mural isn't the only nod to the pilgrimage town. "We also wanted to tie in this lore and the idea of Triboar," adds Riegel. "If you look at the keystones that adorn the top of every arch, as well as on the face of the theater, we have the three carved boars' heads."

WOOD ELF VILLAGE

Simon brings Edgin and Holga into the Neverwinter Wood to meet Doric. Heading to a treetop settlement, the trio try to convince the druid to join their team—something they find all too easy once they mention Forge Fitzwilliam's name. "She seems very uninterested until she finds out what the mission is—which, ultimately, is to take down Forge Fitzwilliam," says Latcham. "He is a bad man who's destroying the Neverwinter Wood, which is where she and the Emerald Enclave live. It's this beautiful wooded area, these giant trees larger than life, this big fantasy world up in the canopies of trees, and Forge is destroying it all. And he has no regard for the environment. He has no regard for these people. He has no regard for their lives."

The treetop village has an otherworldly feel to it. "[This is] another unique environment, something that I've really enjoyed designing," Chan states. "Doric—this is where she lives with the elves, high in the canopy of the trees. . . .

I took inspiration from African trees—the baobab trees—because they're just so handsomely tall. And I imagine that in the rest of the world, Neverwinter Wood would be dwarfed by these humongous baobab trees. And the clever thing with the intertwining, what we call grafting of sycamore trees, is what I decided to base the set design on. And it's something that is quite common, that people do train trees to fuse themselves together, and basically that was the idea of the entire set."

Bridges make travel easier in the forest's canopy. "[This] is based on what we called the living root bridges in India," Chan continues. "It's an organic thing. It's obviously still growing, and probably matures over many, many years. . . . It's something we're going to build on a stage physically with our greens team, and virtually it's interlaced between a canopy of the baobab trees."

Emerald Tavern

The tree grafting found throughout the canopy carries over into the village's interior spaces, like the Emerald Tavern, where various wood elves and members of the Emerald Enclave gather. "I likened the main structure to gardeners who'd spent fifty years grafting tree limbs together," Chan explains. "Like saplings—almost like weaving them—and once they weave, they fuse themselves over many years. So that became the main structure to the tavern itself."

"Whilst the Trip and Shuffle Tavern felt like it was one of those environments where you might get a fair few travelers passing through alongside the regulars propping up the bar, the Emerald Tavern felt much more like a community space, so [it's] a lot lighter, brighter and more welcoming," says Moore. "With it being within a treetop, we wanted to really embrace the idea of nature, so I tried to use things like leaves, seed pods, or flowers for inspiration, if not the natural items themselves. Our lovely greens team scoured the Northern Irish countryside for interesting tree stumps, and then carved them into basic shapes, which our amazing carpenters then sculpted into all the pieces of furniture you see in the set. We also used lotus heads and lilies as inspiration for the design of the little tabletop stove burners, and the large stove at the side of the set. I also found a designer in Canada, Cameron Mathieson, who makes incredible light sculptures from branches and roots wrapped in paper which almost look like twisted leaves or seed pods. He was kind enough to let us use some of his work in the set, which was perfect for the setting."

While VFX was used to create the final look of the village, many of the elements were built practically. "They created a tree and this whole village on top of it in a studio," says Lillis. "I didn't know they were going to do that, but they did. . . . That is one of my favorite sets, especially that tavern that we were in with all of these lights and these branches and there's actual live music playing, and everything. I was thinking, 'Man, Doric lives here? I wish I could live here.'"

MARLAMIN'S COTTAGE

When the group's campaign takes them past the town of Longsaddle, Holga decides the team should make a quick detour to stop by her ex-husband's home. Despite protests, they ride over. Nestled among rolling hills, the team arrives at Marlamin's cottage. The garden is overflowing with vegetation, the shutters have been newly painted, and smoke billows out from the chimney. Everything about this setting is quaint, cozy, and colorful. "Where we shot Marlamin's was absolutely spectacular," acknowledges Peterson. "The mountains and the ridges and the hills that rolled right into the ocean were stunningly beautiful."

All the flowers and plants were strategically placed throughout the garden. "This location is just so perfect for us because it's got natural beauty," states Goldstein. "Ray Chan, our incredible production designer, came and turned it into this magnificent English garden kind of a thing." The sequence at Marlamin's cottage gives audiences a glimpse of the life that Holga once had when she was married. "The Marlamin-Holga relationship was one of the main drivers of me being wanting to be a part of this project," recalls Rodriguez. "The Holga-Marlamin relationship was just, on paper, was so freaking hilarious to me. I was, like, yeah, that kind of reminds me of my love life. It's just so different and awkward and interesting, and I think that's how the heart can be. . . . I was excited to sink my teeth into it. Because I think that love is blind. And I think that it's a beautiful testament to that, and a beautiful metaphor for that—the whole Marlamin and Holga relationship."

EVERMOOR BATTLEFIELD

The adventuring party heads to the Evermoors—the site of a massive battle one hundred years earlier that is now sacred burial ground. Stone cairns act as headstones, dotting the land to mark where fallen barbarians were laid to rest. "The battlefield itself and the build of the cemetery, that was quite a fun build," Chan remembers. "We certainly know that the barbarians don't necessarily have grave markers as such as what we see in our everyday, so [we] did a little bit of research and found that the barbarians sort of bury their dead among these rocks—just, like, hewn rocks, quite organic, not necessarily cut—so I looked around at all the research in the world, and found these cool-looking cairns, which are just standing stones. And so, we had fun just building a whole entire set of cairns with what looks like prehistoric symbolism that represented each dead solider on each cairn."

The entire burial ground was a constructed set. "[The production design] was absolutely incredible," says Smith. "They brought in a bunch of soil and foliage into the soundstage, and you got a fan going, so it felt like we [were] outside, you know, [but] we were inside. It kind of messes with your head a little bit. But then digging up all these corpses and seeing, like, how low this set goes, it was also, like, profound, and you could just tell there was so much artistry."

The barbarians buried here are members of the Uthgardt Elk Tribe, Holga's old clan. "So, this is the sequence it's really cool that we put together," Latcham states. "It takes place in the Evermoor cemetery, which is an ancient cemetery where all of Holga's kinfolk are buried. They were slaughtered there in a fight with a Cult of the Dragon a long, long time ago. And we come to find out that maybe they have the answers to where Mordenkainen's *helm of disjunction* lies. And so that's kind of what takes us to the Evermoors, and it allows us to start digging up all these corpses."

Interrogating the Undead

But how do you get answers from a cadaver? It turns out that if you have the right item, even the dead can talk. One of the artifacts in Simon's possession is a *cleric's token*, which is enchanted with the spell *speak with dead*, allowing the user to revive a corpse to ask them five questions. Once those questions have been asked, the reanimated corpse dies again, unable to be revived a second time. "We think the answer might be in one of these corpses, but there's an entire cemetery full of them, and we don't quite know where to start," explains Latcham of the team's thinking. "And unfortunately, this corpse that we start with does not have all the answers. And we find, as we dig up more and more corpses, that none of them seems to have the answers that we're looking for. And the result is this hilarious blend of action, comedy, a little body horror, and it's just awesome."

The idea for this sequence was there from the beginning. "To give credit where it's due, Michael Gilio, who shares the screenplay credit, that was probably the main thing we kept from his original script because it was such a great idea," says Goldstein. "It felt very D&D. And we changed it around a little bit of how it worked and the questions they asked and the sheer number of corpses."

"It is the most ludicrous and entertaining sequence I'd ever read on a screenplay page," Latcham remembers. "There's just the way the comedy intertwined with the action. The way the guys told the story. It was just hilarious. And, so, to me, bringing that sequence to life and getting the sequence right was super, super important because . . . I've read it, and I've seen it my head, and it's perfect."

"Even as we were going through it in the writing process, you can start to feel the music of the scene, and the fact that it becomes more frenetic and more rapid-fire the longer it goes," recalls Daley. "And so, we knew to complement that we needed something musical that felt unique and walking the line between the absurd, but also the serious, and I think [composer] Lorne Balfe did such an incredible job in walking that line, because the last thing we ever wanted in any of our comedic scenes was comedy music to bolster it, because in our minds, that's the death of comedy."

As the various corpses are brought back to life to tell their stories, audiences are able to witness these past events through the use of flashbacks. "I think any time you get to tell a story through flashbacks in a way that people

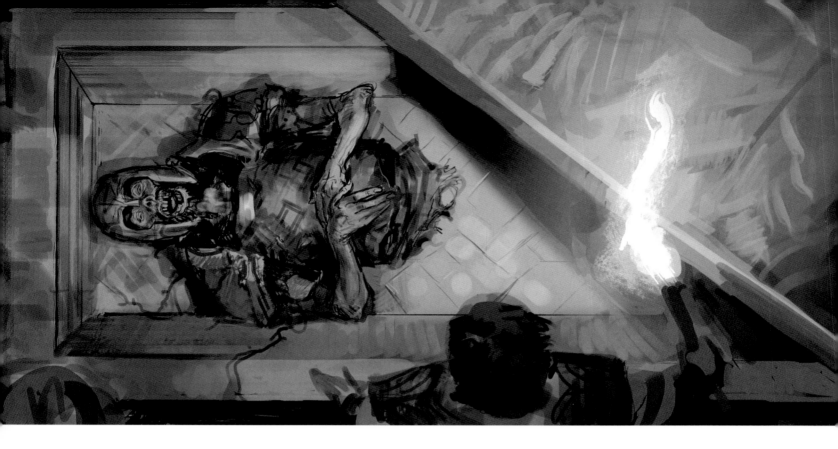

haven't seen before, it's always refreshing," says Daley. "We were taking this relatively trope-y architecture of the flashback storytelling, and the fact that they are limited by five questions and all of their stories end with them dying in different, violent ways, I think [our challenge] was taking the familiar and finding something fresh and new about it. And it also allowed us to really play up that contrast of a super-serious, gritty barbarian battle, juxtaposed with the silliness of these Legacy-creation corpses rattling on about what happened to them."

"I think it's a great mashup of genres in that it's the tragedy of these men's demise, but the absurdity of [that] they're talking corpses and they can only answer five questions and they just flop dead again," adds Goldstein. "I think mashing those two things together is kind of a great opportunity for comedy and tragedy all in one."

To help visualize how the final sequence would work before filming began, storyboards were drawn. These drawings were animated and edited together, creating what is known in Hollywood as an animatic. "Darrin Denlinger, our storyboard artist on this sequence, created the boards that were the first interpretation of this sequence in a visual medium," adds Latcham. "He did such an incredible job of

capturing the timing and the rhythm of the comedy, and it gave us all a ton of confidence that we could bring this to life and make it a truly one-of-a-kind sequence in the film."

"The graveyard sequence was such an inspiring piece of writing, and I could completely visualize it upon the first read of the script," recalls storyboard artist Darrin Denlinger. "Everything was there on the page. The time jumps/transitions were all set in the script and I don't think those elements ever really changed. So the collaboration and brainstorming Zooms with John and Jonathan, Jeremy, and our awesome [director of photography], Barry Peterson, really focused on massaging the material, rather than any wholesale revisions to the sequence. I would say that the first excavated corpse beat took the longest to match the inspiration of the script. Little moments, like Simon tripping and putting his hand through the disgusting, mummified chest of the first corpse, were added to 'plus' what was already there—and a great suggestion from Barry Peterson, doing a triptych of quick grave-digging cuts between each corpse interview, was the cherry on top that immediately gave the sequence a tight, stylistic framework, and allowed each chapter to reset in a fun way."

Evermoor Battlefield Corpses

The drive to shoot practical effects wherever possible extended to the reanimated barbarians. "I think that one of the things the guys have really brought to the table was this desire to make a film that hearkens back to the films of the '80s, and has this really practical underpinning to it," says Latcham. "We're trying to not do everything on bluescreen. We're trying not to do everything with CG. And that sequence, in particular, is a showcase for what practical effects can do. Legacy Effects, led by the great Shane Mahan, is building a whole series of these corpses that we're encapsulating around these wonderful group of actors that we've cast. And there's going to be puppeteering and there's going to be all kinds of rig work, and it's going to be this real great blend of practical and digital effects. And I think it's going to be a real delight for audiences as that sequence comes together."

Six different corpses were created, each with its own unique decomposition. "We built these practical corpses, and so we cast actors that had really specific physical attributes that would allow them to kind of be nearly emaciated enough to seem as if they could fit inside of a corpse's suit," Latcham continues. "And we built these really detailed suits." Those suits—and the actors in them—helped drive the amazing performances captured on camera. "To work with a real corpse, these guys from Legacy who've been around forever and bring this breadth of knowledge and history in our business, that's unbelievable," Pine recalls. "The kind of technical acumen that it takes to do what they do. It's so much fun. . . . It's a mechanical machine. It involves electronics. It involves the making of the costumes, and the mold casting. You're working with an actor that's inside the thing. So just immediately the life inhabited in that piece of art is manifold, rather than just working with [VFX placeholders], which we have done and do in some occasions—the old tennis-ball theory. So, I think it, for me, it heightens the romance of making a film because you feel like you're making a motion picture."

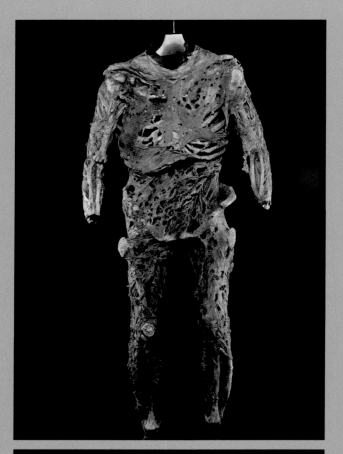

DESSARIN DOCKS

Edgin and his party head toward the fishing village of Mornbryn's Shield, arriving at the River Dessarin's docks. Not only does this location look the part, but it smelled the part too. "They're all so good that sometimes, I remember there was this kind of fish market that we're walking through, and there was actual rotting fish, so it smelled so gross," recalls Smith. "Like squid and stuff. So, I appreciate the authenticity, but that's the price that you have to pay for it. I think the bones were coated in some sort of fish food, or fish, or something like that, but you know, the smell of rotting fish is very similar to the smell of death, so it helps put you in the scene."

HARPERS SANCTUARY

To talk about the Red Wizards in private, Xenk takes Edgin and his crew into a Harpers sanctuary. "They are defenders of justice," says Daley of the Harpers. "And basically, they're a network of spies that work covertly to thwart baddies."

The chamber is decorated with various Harper weapons and emblems. Being in this space makes Edgin uneasy. "He's a Harper who has fallen from grace," Latcham elaborates of Edgin. "He was someone who strove to do good. And when he found out that the salary of a Harper, like what you get for being a Harper, is not really what you probably deserve for being a good guy and trying to protect people and trying to help people, he kind of had questions about that. And he made some decisions that kind of erode his family because he got greedy. I think it's a very common thing in life, right? Like you're trying to do good, but the siren call of doing the other thing comes after you. And so Edgin is someone who's had to deal with this, and had to live with this failure, this mess that

he's caused. . . . And so that is the journey—one of Edgin trying to reunite his family, and trying to live up to the promise that he made, the pledge that he made when he became a Harper."

THAY

Far to the east is Thay, land of the dreaded Red Wizards. "Thay is this terrible, harsh, brutal place off, far from Neverwinter," says Latcham. "It is ruled by a group of zulkirs, who each represent a different form of magic. It's a mag-ocracy. And, so, you have Szass Tam, who's the Zulkir of Necromancy. And at the end of the day, he wants to make everybody undead. He wants to make everybody undead in his image, and he wants all these people to be his undead thralls."

Since seizing control of Thay, Szass Tam has set his sights on other areas in Faerûn, unknown to the citizens of far-off regions. "What we tried to do is establish that there is this underlying conflict that's going on outside of this story that we're primarily focused on," explains Daley. "This dictatorship that's happening in this land of Thay that seems so far away from where our characters are, but ultimately ends up at their doorstep. And so, what we really wanted to allude to is that there was a full story that was taking place throughout that we check in on

occasionally, but don't have the full context for until the third act. And suddenly, they're faced with this thing that they've been sort of ignoring for the first half of the film."

Even in the game, the Red Wizards of Thay are dangerous. "I think the film does a good job of framing them appropriately, which is, left to their own devices, they will do terrible things," says Jarvis. "They will conscript people into un-death, and they will use extremely powerful magics to get their way. Szass Tam was always in the script— not really as the main villain, but the villain behind the villain behind the villain. Like, you have that kind of nested-doll of badness in the film of Forge, and then you realize, Sofina is really pulling the strings, and then you see that there's something even bigger behind Sofina."

THE UNDERDARK

HIDDEN BENEATH THE surface of Faerûn is a vast system of tunnels and caverns called the Underdark. Danger abounds in this subterranean network, with death lurking around every rocky corner and crag. One thing is certain—there is no greater dungeon in all of D&D than the Underdark. "The Underdark is really dangerous primarily because of the source of creatures that live in there," suggests Jarvis. "You could also fall. Just the physical danger of the terrain. The unironic darkness of the Underdark can also be a challenge, and then the things you encounter are what make it very dangerous. And it's not like there's a hospital around every street corner, so if you get into trouble in the Underdark, you're in trouble."

Xenk leads Edgin and the others into the Underdark through a secret entrance in the Kryptgarden Forest—one of the many entrances hidden throughout Faerûn. "There's multiple ways to enter," says Jarvis of the cavernous web, "but who could [possibly] know all of the crevices that could eventually lead to the Underdark?" After entering the Underdark, Xenk continues his role as guide, escorting everyone through the cavern in something the filmmakers called the Underdark journey. "It's just challenge after challenge, adventure after adventure, as our characters weave their way through the Underdark," claims Latcham. "It makes for this really great central set-piece in the film. And it captures this dungeon crawl kind of vibe. And you get to go on this journey with them as they make their way through the Underdark. . . . And so, you get to go on these quests, and then the fun of the movie is trying to figure out how to make each of these quests, because each quest is like its own little mini movie that you have to try to sort out. Like, how do we actually achieve this giant dragon chase? How do we achieve this

giant bridge sequence? How do we achieve this intellect-devourers scene? . . . It's all these different sequences, they're each their own quest in and of itself that have to be designed. You have to come up with puzzles and gags and creatures. And so, the movie allows you just to journey through a big swath of the D&D lore and experience all kinds of creatures."

Multiple sets were constructed to film the scenes in the Underdark. "This was built on two stages," explains Chan. "The Underdark was built on a soundstage and revamped twice, so we got value out of the set—whereas the Dolblunde and the Terracotta Valley [set] was built on one of the larger stages. . . . We can't build the entire set, but we built enough for the actors, and the visual effects team would then enhance [in post]."

"The idea in the initial days for the Underdark was that it was all CG—and a lot of it, of course, was—but I don't like that," says Stewart. "I don't believe that it's fair. In the blue screen world, it's, 'Here. Love this tennis ball on a stick. You love this.' You know? It's just so horrible. So I was fighting as much as I could to get as much physical set as possible. . . . It's important that it not just be a logistical convenience, or a financial convenience. You've got to consider, 'What does the cast feel the first time they see it? And how do they feel spending days in there? Are they getting something through osmosis from the environment?' I believe they do. . . . The Underdark was the one [set] that I think I fought to have as much tactile, actual set as we could possibly afford, and I think that really made a difference for the cast. And I think their ability to see it in their mind's eye as they were shooting it."

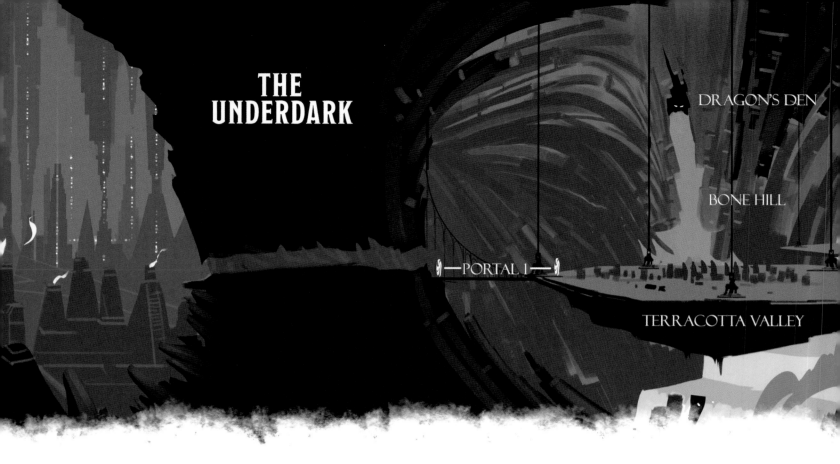

THE UNDERDARK

DRAGON'S DEN

BONE HILL

—PORTAL 1—

TERRACOTTA VALLEY

TUNNELS AND CLIFFS

To design the tunnels and cliffs of the Underdark, the filmmakers looked to Mother Nature for guidance. "One day, I had this inspirational thought that, why don't we just riff off real world where we have shifting plates, tectonic plates, where the earth's core is always constantly shifting—hence you get tsunamis and earthquakes," recalls Chan. "So, the first drop-in cavern is where we have the, what I called fingers, and this is our very first journey into the Underdark. . . . The look of the cave itself is something I grabbed out of my brain, which was based on the stone forest in China, in fact, Madagascar as well, where a lot of the rock formations basically deteriorate vertically. So, I literally turned it on its head, and had all the stone structure facing horizontally."

It's hard to see underground. Thankfully, native species use their phosphorescence to help light the way. "They start in a cavern," says Chan of the adventuring party. "And then as they travel through these tunnels out of the cavern, they come across these biolumi, which are creatures that supposedly react to our heroes as they walk past them."

"[The biolumi] come alive as they sense the humans, and then sort of fall back into hibernation," explains Chan.

DOLBLUNDE

DEAD END CHAMBER

SEE-SAW BRIDGE

DRAGON

PORTAL 2

CHASE ON AQUEDUCT

DOLBLUNDE

Eventually the team arrives on the outskirts of Dolblunde, the ruins of an ancient city that was once home to thousands of gnomes. Around the metropolis, dangling platforms span volcanic chasms, acting as pathways above the boiling lava. The inclusion of these swinging platforms was inspired by one of the director's own experiences. "There was a campaign I was in where our players got stuck on a platform in this pit that was suspended by chains," recalls Daley. "It gave us the idea to have this city that they visit in the Underdark be this series of massive platforms suspended by huge, car-sized chain-links."

Although Dolblunde appears abandoned, one resident remains—a large red dragon. "There's the bridge, there's the accidental collapse, and that is a very hot lava underworld with hanging platforms above the lava," says Giorgiutti of Dolblunde. "Who knows? The platforms may have come about because the lava from below has melted into whatever earth was there before, and now there's these hanging, swinging platforms. And then you have the hill of bones, which is where we reveal our dragon. And all of the dragon chase then happens within the hanging platform and an aqueduct, and it's all lit with this river of lava."

The cave's geology is different around Dolblunde. Chan explains, "For the cave vaults, I looked at the Giant's Causeway in Ireland, but also there's many basalt structures in Fingal's Cave in Scotland, and also in Iceland. We feel that the earth's tremendous forces can force the basalt fingers upward this time, and again, giving the set a cool lighting environment. I thought it would be really cool for the lava, rather than have lava at the base of the plates, the lava's leaching out of cracks, almost like a volcano—an

active volcano—and so that it would spurt out and just die away, and spurt out again."

It is here that our heroes find what they have been seeking. "This is the Underdark in Dolblunde," says Chan. "This is a huge part of DUNGEONS & DRAGONS in our movie because it is where Xenk is the link to find the *helm of disjunction*."

Xenk has hidden the helmet in a field of warrior statues. "I had invented this sea of this dead army of gnomes, and they're literally based on the terracotta soldiers in China," Chan reveals. "These are what we call the Terracotta Valley. They're about eight feet tall. They have been sculpted by our sculpting team, and built like a Greek column, so they're sectionalized. . . . Terracotta Valley was never scripted. It was just something I thought was a cool thing where you could have this silent army,

some standing, some kneeling, but all carrying a bowl because they were bearing gifts paying homage to the dragon."

One specific statue is the keeper of the helmet. "I thought of this crazy cool way of revealing the helmet, which is just this—almost like a puzzle board in itself, which is actually hidden," says Chan. "It could be hidden among a thousand, five thousand different bowls, it's just that Xenk knows exactly which one to go to."

Aqueduct

on lair

terracotta valley

Hill of bones

Bridge into Dolblunde

"IF THESE RUNE WORDS BE REVEALED,
YOU'LL FIND THE ANAGRAM THAT LIES CONCEALED.
A CRYPTIC MEANING IT MAY YIELD,
OF AN OBJECT ONE CAN WIELD.
THE ITEM WON'T BE FAR AFIELD,
FOR WITH IT YOUR PATH SHALL BE UNSEALED."

HE TWISTING RUNES INSCRIBED HEREIN
LEAD ONE AWAY AND

BACK AGAIN TURN THE PLATE MARKED
"LEFT" RIGHT THRICE WHILE

UP

LEFT

RIGHT

DOWN

AND SLIDES RIGHT HOME
DOWN" SHOULD BE LEFT WELL ALONE.

"RIGHT" SHOULD TURN LEFT ONLY
"UP" SPEAKS TRUE

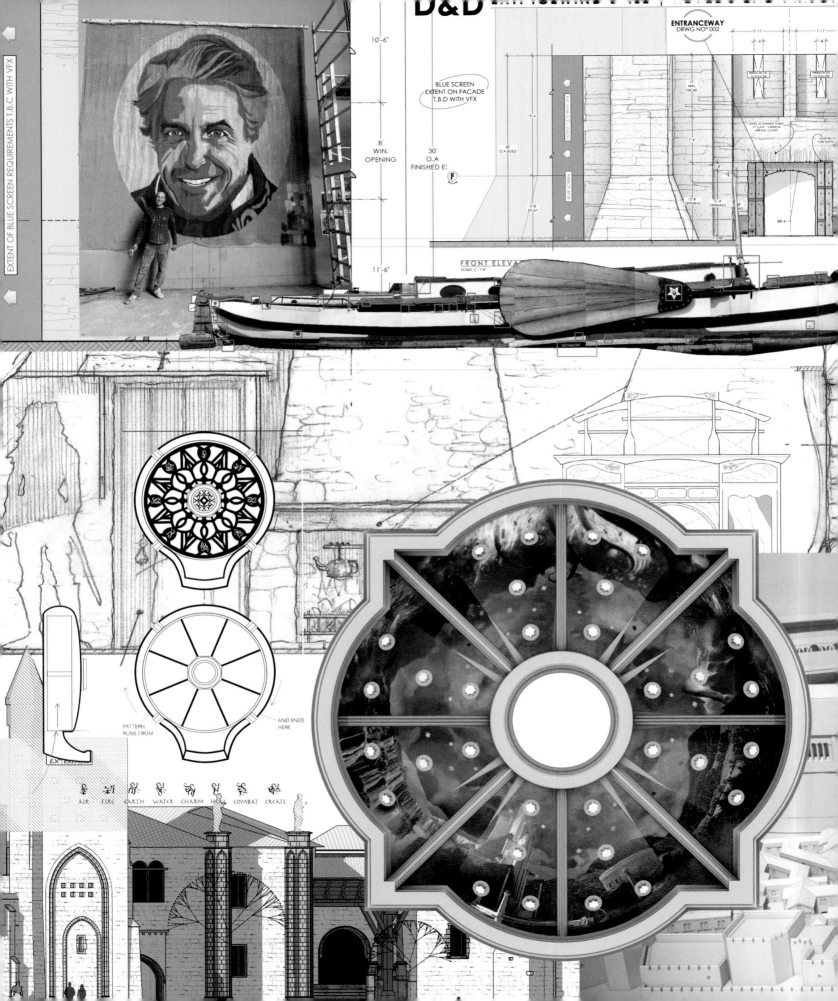

D&D

BLUE SCREEN
EXTENT ON FACADE
T.B.D WITH VFX

10'-6"

8'
WIN.
OPENING

30'
O.A
FINISHED E:

11'-6"

30
O.A BUILD

19'-4

10'-8"
SPLAY

12'-8"
OPENING

FRONT ELEVA
SCALE: 2" = 1'-0"

AIR   FIRE   EARTH   WATER   CHARM   HEAL   COMBAT   CREATE

PATTERN
RUNS FROM

AND ENDS
HERE

EXTERIOR

[4]

THE MAGIC OF FILMMAKING

LIGHTS. CAMERA. ACTION!

DURING YOUR CAMPAIGN, you will come across decision points in which the DM has you roll dice to determine the outcome of your choices. You may want to parkour up the side of a building and sneak into a second-story window, but a roll will determine whether your infiltration is successful, or you end up flat on your back—alerting the guards in the process.

While the film doesn't have dice, that doesn't mean our heroes are always successful at achieving their goals. "There's no allusions to playing the game, but the characters have to make decisions much in the way that they would if they were playing the game," says Goldstein. "They're presented with situations and challenges, and they have to find innovative, clever ways to deal with the problem. And then their success or failure, while no dice are actually rolled, it plays out in a way that feels like it could come out of a game."

"There are a lot of mistakes that our characters make, much like the characters in gameplay," states Daley. "A lot of pivoting, a lot of thinking on your feet, and figuring out other ways into a plan where it didn't work out the first way. And we really wanted to embrace that, and it also allows for a more fluid kind of storytelling that keeps audiences guessing."

"Also, a good Dungeon Master pulls the rug out from his players quite often," adds Goldstein. "And that's—you think you're going down a certain road, and then it's not at all what you expected [as a player], and that's one of the things we tried to do in the movie."

Translating Page to Screen

The character decisions conceived were wild and original. Now a singular question remained: How would they film those sequences? "The taking something from the page that you've been sitting with and imagining for however many months that we'd been working on it, and finally

seeing it realized takes a moment to process," notes Daley. "There were times when we were writing the script and we were like, 'Can you imagine actually shooting this moment? How insane would that be?' And then on the day, when we're doing it, of course, we're now just swarmed with thoughts of how we're going to cover it and get it all done in time. But there is that sense of just pinching yourself at how big and spectacular it all is."

The Logistics of Creativity

Producers dealing with operational logistics are needed to back up creative teams, and on a film this large, having the right person fulfilling this role was crucial. "Denis Stewart, the executive producer on the film, had a huge task with trying to mount this production," says Latcham. "He was able to give Ray Chan and Ben Snow everything that we needed to really bring this film to life. It was an epic task, especially in the midst of the pandemic, and Denis and his incredible team did a wonderful job."

"The creative producers dream it, and I make it," says Stewart. "I'm a logistician. They bring me their vision and their ideas, and then I say, 'Okay. Off to the drawing board. I'll be back.' And then I literally go to a drawing board—I'm a whiteboard nut—where I can gather people around, and just organize things. . . . I have a creative contribution, but that has to be earned through the trust of the directors and the creative producers learning that I have their best interests at heart, because it's not always a dollar-for-dollar conversation. It has to be, first, what does it look like? What is best? And then you start to evaluate the cost to it. . . . Every creative person, they just want it all. And so you have to manage them, and help them to pick and choose which moments really seat with the audience. Where's the bang for the buck? And it takes time. It takes time to listen to them closely. Not crush their dreams for the longest of times,

but yet not lead them into false hope that they're going to get everything that they want."

Both of these producer types are needed to complete a film—with a firm partnership helping to make a hard shoot a little bit easier. "I love Jeremy Latcham," exclaims Stewart. "He said a couple of times, 'This is probably the hardest movie I've ever worked on.' But you can't faze him. He just keeps going. He's determined, and he's smart. He's learned so much over his career, and he's got a great instinct. He really, really does. And he's such a partner for me. He helps me help him. And if he needs help, man, I'll go to the end of the world to get it for him."

Practical Effects

While visual effects were needed to execute the filmmakers' vision, if something could be shot practically, it was. "Our philosophy has been to avoid as much blue and green screen as we possibly can," Daley continues. "That said, there is a great deal of it for the scope that we need to capture."

"It helps me as a filmmaker to see something . . . to have something tangible," adds Peterson. "Something you can touch, something you can feel helps everybody. I think that you understand what film you're making at that point. Obviously, things get polished in visual effects later, but I think the ability to see something live helps everybody."

Whether the effects of spellcasting, or creature attacks and transformations, these were the kinds of things that were brought to life through the magic of filmmaking.

REVEL'S END ESCAPE

Two years into their sentence at Revel's End, Edgin and Holga go before the Absolution Council to plead their case. While Edgin could have used his charisma to charm the Council for early release, his actual plan is for him and Holga to grab Jarnathan—the one Council member who can fly—push him out of the window, and have him glide the duo both down safely. "The scenes in the Absolution Council were really exciting," says Goldstein. "To see it come to life in this beautiful set with these amazing prosthetic builds, and creatures, and then to hear Edgin tell his tale of woe and his backstory, and they jump out of the window like that—almost exactly as we imagined it—and to be able to turn your vision into reality in that way is really gratifying."

To bring the sequence to life, the special-effects team built a window for everyone to pass through. "We basically built this eight-foot-diameter ornate window with stone mullions and all that sort of thing," Conway recalls. "So that's all breakaway [glass]—totally breakaway—and smash, out, there you go. And thankfully you've got a camera inside and a camera outside so you catch [the action] as much as possible. But it was one of those things that doing breakaway glass is fine, but when you got breakaway glass that's [in] those sort of [ornate] shapes, it's putting that in [place]. We did a night shift and it took us eight hours to put in, and it was a real trembler as well, out there on a scissor lift, which is moving around everywhere, and trying to stow this glass."

Another major element that was needed for the sequence involved Jarnathan, the aarakocra, who ended up as a blend of practical and visual effects. "He's the fourth councillor that they meet at Revel's End and he's a Legacy [Effects] suit," says Snow. "He's got articulated beaks, he's got these wings that actually span, and then, he walks around on—he's got claw feet and hands and such—but we do a little bit of digital work to clean up some rig, because he's got these stilts he has to walk on. . . . And then, when the characters decide that they're going to [escape]—he's their way out of jail. They're going to grab him and smash their way out to freedom, and they all fall. And there's a lot of stunt work. Then we add those wings in computer graphics, so we've got some beautiful reference from what the Legacy guys made that we use in the council chamber, but . . . we have the flexibility of the computer graphics [to add elements] once they start falling and flying across the Icelandic landscape."

Edgin and Holga's escape from Revel's End is the first major sequence in the film. "That moment is a good tone-setter for the film, because you do have a fantastical humanoid that you don't see in general fantasy, and you have that moment of characters trying something that probably shouldn't work, and it does," says Jarvis. "Those are the kind of memorable moments that *do* come out of the gameplay. Of a player saying, 'I'm going to jump on this thing and push it out the window and see if we can kind of glide down.' And the Dungeon Master is like, 'Okay, man. Roll.' And it's like, 'Oh, shit. That worked!' I don't know what that [roll] would have been as I'm not the gameplay guy. I don't know that it was a twenty, but they rolled high."

QUICKSAND FLOOR

When Edgin and Holga confront Forge for the first time, the heroes find themselves in a precarious situation when Sofina traps the two of them in the floor. "[A] spell that's really fun is a moment early in the film, when Sofina takes the ground and turns it into, basically, not ground," says Latcham. "We built this version of the ground, and our special-effects guy, Sam Conway, was able to figure out how to take sand, and, in an instant, liquefy it. And so, he takes a box full of sand, like a glass box full of sand, he gets the certain kinds of sand, and he fills it with air from an air cannon really quickly. And then by filling with air, it turns from being [something] hard that you can stand on to being liquid. It doesn't make any sense to me. I just don't understand the physics of it, but he shows us a test for this and I'm, like, 'Holy cow. That's the spell that's in the book. You just did that. Are you a magician?' And he was like, 'No, I'm the special-effects guy.'"

"That was one of the earliest ones that we tackled because I knew it probably, potentially, would be one of the hardest ones," remembers Conway of Sofina's *transmute rock* spell. "I did a bit of research on that, and a few experiences that me and my father [special-effects supervisor Richard Conway] discovered in previous jobs. But

effectively, we are making quicksand—instant quicksand—so the sand would be the solid surface and then we aerate it, and it loses all its bounce, and they just sink straight through it."

To set up the beginning of the sequence, the filmmakers laid out small tiles in the shape of a Neverwinter-inspired crest, seamlessly blending into the rest of the floor. "We spent a lot of time trying to work out how to put the tiles over it so it would look like it was an intact set piece," explains Conway. "And then with the flick of a switch, we introduced the air and then the actors just sank straight through the tile, straight into the sand. It looked great and it was good."

The way the trick worked was kept from the actors for filming. "We bring that [gag] onto the set, and we don't really let the actors try it ahead of time," recalls Latcham. "The actors, we just tell them to get up and walk across the set, and they do so, and Sam liquefies the ground. And it turns from being sand in a solid state to . . . all of a sudden, the actors are sinking in it. And the looks on their faces are so like they're unsure of what the heck just happened to them. And you get this moment in Forge's office where all the reactions are really, really real as a result."

PLAYHOUSE REVERSE GRAVITY

Simon's wild magic is first put on display in the Triboar playhouse, where an unruly crowd prompts him to cast a self-defense spell—which backfires in a spectacular way. "So, for the crowd in Triboar, he does the flame-finger [*firefinger*] spell, which is just exactly what it sounds like, he just lights his finger on fire," says Smith. "He does the fresh-cut-grass-smell spell, which is just making the air smell like fresh-cut grass. And then, when things get heated, he tries to do a *shield spell* but ends up reversing gravity so everyone flies up in the air, but that is the beauty of wild magic, of being a wild-magic sorcerer."

To film this sequence, the filmmakers didn't rely on camera angles, or a rotating set. "We built two versions of the set," says Latcham. "One was right-side up. One was upside down. We rigged people [up]. We had the largest collection of winches and pulleys that I've ever seen in my life, all computerized so we could take all the stunt people—pull them up, drop them down, pull them up, drop them down—and everyone could be kind of flying through the air. And it was all in the service of this one gag. So upside-down photography, flipping things upside down, stunt-work rigging, it was madness. All to make this magical spell feel real. And, so, we actually had to do all this movie magic to make the magic in the movie feel like real magic that actually existed. . . . It was a real pain in the butt to shoot, but it's worth it, because you look at it and you're like, 'That feels like gravity was actually reversed in that room. How the heck did they do that?'"

OWLBEAR TRANSFORMATION

Deep within the Neverwinter Wood, a wood elf is accused of treason by Forge Fitzwilliam. The sentence—death by public execution. Luckily, Doric is ready for a rescue. "She transforms—from a horse into an owlbear—and saves a wood elf in peril," says second-unit VFX supervisor Kevin Cahill.

To film the owlbear transformation sequence, the filmmakers captured elements on set to help VFX artists complete the final effect. "The owlbear scene is broken up into a number of parts," explains Daley. "Basically, people reacting to nothing, people reacting to a guy in a silly jumpsuit, and then clean plates, where we don't even have our people [in the scene]. And then that's all taken to the geniuses at our visual-effects department."

"The owlbear's a challenging creature," says Snow. "What we do with something like that is research it a lot. We worked a lot on the designs. . . . The directors decided that they wanted a snowy owl as the basis for the owlbear. They are very keen to anchor this into reality, so we got lots of pictures of snowy owls and then we actually were able to borrow an owl as a reference, and we also just had some feathers that we could use as reference. And then, we had a stunt guy dressed in a white costume. Now, obviously, he's not as big as an owlbear, but [he's there] just so we can have something that will tell the animators later on [where to animate], and the editors when they're trying to edit this [scene]. It's not just a bunch of people acting against a tennis ball. You actually see a guy go through the motions. . . . So that's the first time we meet Doric. She's this owlbear and that'll be a big combination of background plates and, of course, computer graphics that [VFX company] Industrial Light & Magic's going to do."

DORIC CASTLE ESCAPE

Edgin and his team recruit Doric to infiltrate Castle Never. They hope that she can stealthily uncover intel from within the castle's walls. Unfortunately, her wild shape—a fly—is detected by Red Wizard Sofina, beginning an escape sequence that leads Doric out of the castle and straight through the city of Neverwinter—all seemingly captured in one single shot. "It was one of the first sequences that we devised when we pitched the movie to the studio," recalls Daley. "Before we even wrote the script, we loved the idea of following this character as they transformed in a single shot, because it's something that we had never seen before. And there's also something inherently immersive in the nature of one-ers. It's why we have that egg chase [scene] in [the film] *Game Night*, and it's really fun and really successful when you can pull it off."

Even though the sequence appears to be done in one shot, the process to film it, like many of the sequences in the film, was arduous. "I don't know that either of us knew the technological complexity of making a movie like this, as fully as we came to learn," claims Goldstein. "You were often shooting one sequence in three different places over three different weeks, and it's incredibly specific. It's how high is the camera from the ground, and what angle is it pointed in this shot? It's got to match on the B side, or it won't cut. That kind of thing. In this, that was especially true of that Doric one-er. We shot it to be a fake single shot. . . . It's going to be pretty amazing, but it was a bear to shoot."

With several transformations throughout the entirety of the sequence, it was apparent that computer graphics would be heavily involved. "She ends up using a lot of different tricks in the book to transform," Snow says of Doric. "There's an extended sequence where she's racing through the castle and has to change to different creatures to evade capture. And so, in that case, she's going to go from as small as a fly up to a hawk. . . . Then she becomes a cat, and a dog at one point. And then, as with the owlbear where we had a stuntman pretending to be the owlbear so we could have that, we had someone playing Doric as a deer—and it was a parkour guy—and so, he was incredibly agile, fast, was able to run through the streets. [A] really, really cool and talented stuntman, and it really helps give us real, dynamic [movement] for the crowd to react to, for the camera to react to. We all understand what's going on. It's a guy in a brown suit, and he's not running on all fours, but he's able to leap on buildings because he's a parkour guy. And you get the feel, and it really helps us then when we go to our visual-effects team."

This sequence allows Doric to shine. "In many ways, she is our Hulk," Daley suggests. "She is this diminutive, soft-spoken character that really comes into her own when she's changing into these creatures. So, you get to see the whole gamut of her personality expressed through the different creatures that she becomes."

To turn a large sequence like Doric's escape into reality, someone is needed to orchestrate the various departments into harmonious balance. "A film with this many huge sequences means a ton of preparation and planning and a lot of that intensive work fell onto [executive producer] Denis Stewart and [unit production manager] John Naclerio's shoulders," says Latcham. "They really corralled a giant team under difficult, pandemic circumstances to bring these huge action sequences to life."

THEMBERCHAUD ESCAPE

Deep in the Underdark, Xenk fights Dralas and his Thayan assassins. With his masterful swordsmanship, the paladin strikes them all down. But the victory is short-lived. These Thayans are part of the undead, and will quickly rise again. Xenk, Edgin, and the rest of the team—with helmet in hand—rush toward the only exit they see. "The only way out would be walking toward the hill of bones—which, funnily enough, the guys don't realize is a hill of bones, because at the bottom of the bowl, the bottom of the hill is sort of sandy because the bones have been there for a while, and have decomposed almost like to sand," says Chan.

The filmmakers had to get creative to find a material for constructing the hill of bones. "The hill of bones absolutely reeked of fish because the bones were mostly ground-up seashells," recalls Page. "Throughout that entire scene, everyone is acting with the overwhelming smell of sea bones, which is lovely." As the party rushes up the hill, they are soon confronted by what caused the bone pile—a ferocious and hungry dragon called Themberchaud. "The reveal of him is really important," Giorgiutti states. "He's a serious dragon, and he's super-angry. And he wants more food. And yes, he lives on a hill of bones, which essentially is the bones of all the people, other creatures, and what have you, that he's eaten."

An Unexpected Dragon

The hill of bones was the first major part in the Themberchaud escape sequence. "We're running up the mountain—hill of bones, I think they call it—and upon that run, there's a massive dragon up at the top of the hill," recalls Rodriguez. "And the dragon . . . it blows at us. And as it blows at us, the force of its breath blows all of us off the hill of bones. And so, we're on, like, a good 75-degree angle, I'd have to assume, and we're on wires. And we have to run up. And as soon as we run up, we get jerked back, and we all go flying in midair."

"We hit all the actors with an air cannon, and put them all on these wire rigs," explains Daley. "Our stunt team said that they had never put so many primary actors in one rig, and one wire stunt, in their entire careers. It was probably needlessly ambitious, considering the shot lasts only a few seconds, but I think any time you can put your actors in those situations and not rely on stunt people to do it, you can see it. It shows."

Although a fire dragon, Themberchaud has trouble producing a flame. "With Themberchaud, he's supposed to be so morbidly obese that his sparking mechanism is broken in his throat," says Snow. "He actually can't ignite his gas breath—he's just got these sparks. It's like when a gas ignition breaks on the stove top."

A lack of spark doesn't mean he's not dangerous. Themberchaud easily devours Dralas and the Thayan assassins before setting off in pursuit of the others. Edgin and our group start to run, darting through Dolblunde as fast as they can. If they aren't quick enough, they know they're next on the menu. "The scene is just one big cat-and-mouse chase now," says Chan. "You've got a dragon, which is about one hundred twenty feet long, slightly overweight, chasing a more nimble group of heroes, but ultimately he's also fearsome. And it's a fun chase because he's causing mayhem and chaos as he's crashing through aqueducts, and viaducts—and the guys are just a couple of centimeters, a couple of inches, ahead of the snapping jaws."

"I treated him like a creature we can relate to," says storyboard artist David Krentz of Themberchaud. "Like when he slides down the hill [of bones], that was essentially a penguin sliding down an ice slope. When he was running and stumbling into things, I was thinking of a corgi with really short legs skittering across a smooth floor and it can't stop, bumping into things. And sometimes, when his huge momentum couldn't be stopped, I thought of an elephant seal or sea lion rolling around. Being ambulatory is not this thing's forte."

The adventuring party jumps onto a suspended platform, careful to stay away from both the dragon's mouth and the bubbling lava below. "The whole set, the whole environment is supposed to be hanging on chains," Conway confirms. "A few of the chains break, so all these platforms are moving around inside this space. So, we built a sixty-foot-by-twenty-foot gimbal—like a

teeter rig. . . . This [gimbal] was specifically designed for what we call the seesaw bridge where the dragon jumps on one end and it teeters over, and it makes them slide down toward the dragon. So that was designed specifically for that."

The gimbal wasn't the only aspect the filmmakers worried about when executing the scene. "It's very complicated," adds Conway. "[There's] fire effects in there, and there's a lot of moving parts, and that was one of those sequences I was pleased to finish and get past because that was a real soak of [both] mental capacity, and physical."

Eventually the dragon chases the team into a cave. Although Themberchaud can fit only his head in the space, there is no way out. Writhing, the dragon begins to destroy the tiny chamber, escalating the danger within the space. "The dragon chases them into the end of this alley, and it's basically a little cave," Conway continues. "The dragon can't get [in] any farther, but it decides to smash the cave up. And it turns out that the cave is underwater—under the ocean—and as it bangs its head around, [it] starts opening up fissures, and slowly the cave fills up [with water]."

The filmmakers needed to find the best way to film this suddenly aquatic space. "Aside from all the other stuff that we do, water plays a big part, and it did, in this tunnel—this dead-end alley," explains Conway. "This cave was filling up with water, but very, very quickly, you know? And to do that, you can't just pump water in. The pumps you'd need [to do that] are gargantuan. So, it's better to sink the set, so we sunk the set into a tank of water. At the same time, we had lots of larger pumps pumping fissures through the roof and stuff like that. There was plenty of water working there, and as far as an effect, water is fantastic."

With nowhere to go and the chamber's air supply in jeopardy, a quick plan is devised by Edgin to create an explosion using Themberchaud's gas and Simon's flaming-finger trick—a cantrip that can't trigger the effects of the sorcerer's wild magic. "Themberchaud traps our heroes in a big watery cavern, and it's up to Simon to pull off a trick and save the day," says Latcham. "Ed[gin]'s quick thinking is going to be what gets us out of the jam."

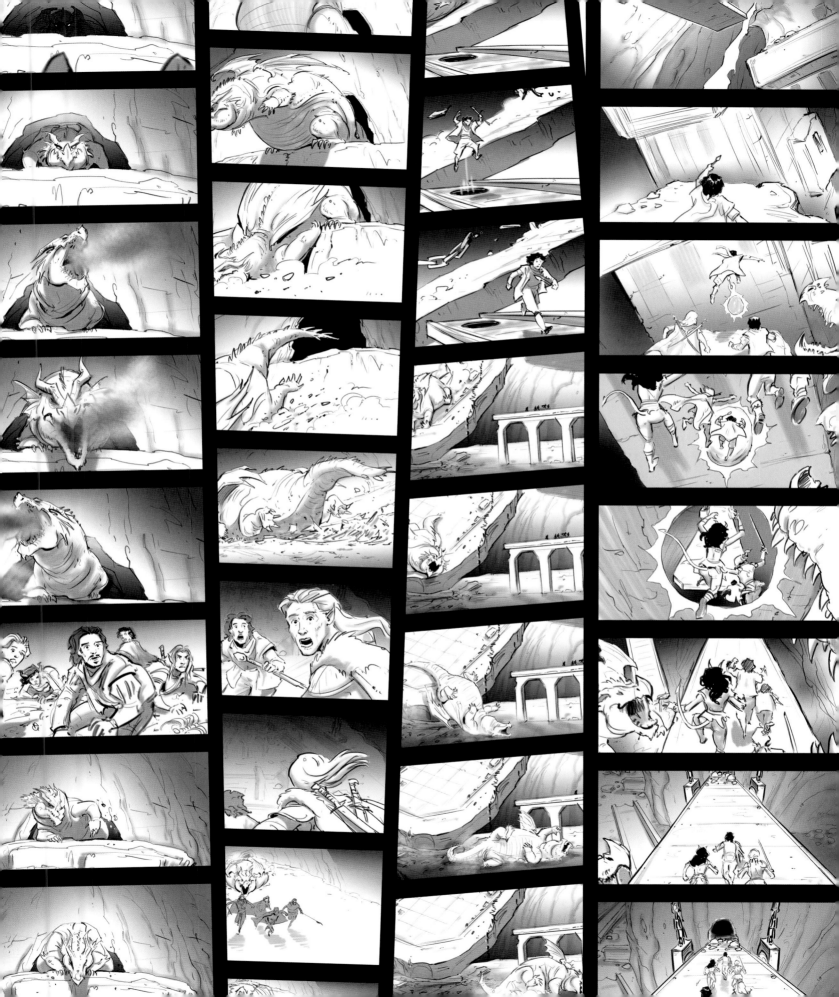

PORTAL HEIST

Simon is struggling to attune to the *helm of disjunction*. Worrying he won't master it in time to help the team break into the Castle Never vault, a plan B is formed. To avoid having to directly break the arcane seal protecting the vault, they devise a way to go around it using Simon's *hither-thither staff*. The plan is to create a portal on an artifact—a portrait in this case—and get others to place it into the vault. Then, once the portrait is within the vault's chamber, they can transport themselves directly inside.

Edgin heads to a local merchant's to buy a fake piece of treasure to plant in the carriage—a framed portrait that, to the untrained eye, is of a seemingly random nobleman. The painting is actually of Volothamp "Volo" Geddarm, a character in DUNGEONS & DRAGONS known as the ultimate source of information on all things within the realm. "I believe it was [concept artist] Wes[ley] Burt who painted that Volo portrait," says Jarvis. "It is recognizably Volo. He has that signature hat. Kind of an Italian almost Renaissance-y sort of garb is how it generally presents. But again, that's another example of fans in the know will be like, 'Oh, that's Volo,' but to brand-new people it's just a fancy painting of someone who was probably important."

The team waits on a hill outside of Neverwinter, waiting for a treasure carriage to come down the high road. Eventually, a team of horses approach, drawing a large carriage behind them. "We're looking at the Fenn's treasure carriage, which is what I call, like, an armored cash truck, really cashbox, on wheels," says Chan. "I was working on a movie in India, and I just happened to be in a small city. It was about five thousand years old, between Mumbai and Hampi, and I was taken to a town square where I saw a stone-built chariot, which has stuck in my mind. . . . It's multifaceted, and this thing was about fifteen feet tall. [And I thought] I've got to get that in a movie one day. And so, the treasure carriage was born. Whereas this one, this has to move. It has to be a practical picture vehicle. So, all the chassis is structural. Even a vehicle of this size, it's got its own disc-brake system, and it's one hell of a carriage."

With the treasure carriage in sight, the team needs to work both quickly and stealthily for this plan to work. The adventuring party uses a series of portals to sneak onto the treasure carriage to plant their portrait.

Portal Physics

Filming this sequence required immense planning. "Which way was up, which way was down, how we were looking from one portal into another space five hundred yards down the road just was a bit of a mind-blowing thing to figure out," recalls Giorgiutti. "There's a lot of pieces to this moving puzzle. So, the portals were definitely something that sounds simple, but on this film, it's probably one of the more complex things we have in terms of shooting." Multiple settings were used, adding to the intricacy of the shoot. "That was another piece that some of it was done on stage, some of it was done out on location," adds Goldstein. "We built that wagon interior, so the door—so the whole wall—could open out so our camera could go around her [Doric] when she comes inside, and it was a complex bit of business, but it's also super fun."

"It was a really interesting sequence in that it started a little bit smaller than it ended up," recalls Snow. "It took a lot of planning and a bunch of charts and diagrams and stuff to show everyone where what was going to be filmed where, and that sort of thing. And it was really hard even for me, and I probably knew the sequence better than anyone, to just get your head around. . . . The hope was by doing as much pre-planning and being as careful in the shoot as we could, that we'd make it a little bit easier in post, and certainly make it more possible to make it look real. And as you're shooting, of course, you run into all sorts of elaborate things. . . . It was just this elaborate choreography of the different departments working together, but by doing it that way, we were able to get it pretty much all in camera except for the transition part."

For the filmmaking team, the keys to creating this extremely challenging sequence were trust and communication. "The portal heist sequence is a sequence that to John and Jonathan was always 100 percent clear to them in their heads," says Latcham. "They knew exactly what they wanted out of the sequence, and the challenge became trying to communicate that vision to everybody, because the way they saw it unfolding was so complex and intricate that no one [could] quite grasp what we were doing, even as we were doing it. But somehow John and Jonathan, the entire time, knew exactly what we were doing. And so, the special-effects guys, and the visual-effects guys, and the DP [director of photography], and me, and the production designer are all standing around going, 'Wait, so what's this piece? So we're going to shoot it upside down and she's going to come through, and then we're going to be up. And you want the set to open? And the set is going to flip open on the side? Okay. I think I understand.'" And John and Jonathan were, like, 'Yeah, yeah, yeah, trust us. All right. Now, action.' And we do it and we're looking at it and we're like, I just don't understand. And so the whole time this kept happening. And we send the footage off to LA, to the editor, and the editor calls me and he's like, 'I don't understand the footage.' And I said, 'I don't know, but John and Jonathan see it 100 percent clearly in their head. We'll get to it when we start cutting. I'm sure we'll make it work. It's all going to make sense.' And it turns out that John and Jonathan knew exactly what they were doing because the sequence turned out awesome."

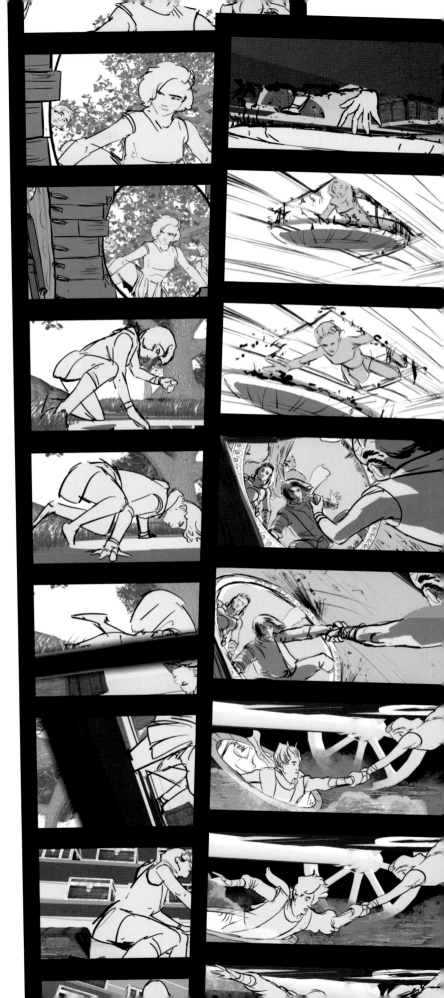

HOLGA ARMORY BATTLE

When the team breaks into Castle Never, Holga gets a chance to showcase her barbarian rage against a group of guards. "In the armory, Holga has an incredible fight that we're going to get to see where she [has access to] all these half-built weapons," says Latcham. "She's fighting her way through with a hilt of a sword, and a half-done mace, and all kinds of stuff. It's going to be really fun."

By taking place in a blacksmith's armory, the unfinished weapons around were a huge source of inspiration for the fight. "The set was amazing," says fight choreographer Georgi Manchev. "It was so rich of, 'We can do a lot of different kinds of stuff around it,' like playing with the chain, playing with the different type of hammers, mace, swords, axe, shields. So, you can actually use everything."

Holga stands her ground against twenty men. "We liked the idea of taking the gender roles that you would imagine in an adventure movie like this, and flipping them on their head," says Daley. "Letting the female character be the one that's the brute—the one that fights and asks questions later."

"[The] armory fight was one of the biggest fights in the movie," claims stunt coordinator Dian Hristov. "It's [an] incredible set, incredible environment there, and we used all possible weapons and stuff around to fight with all these guys."

"Dian Hristrov and his team of Bulgarian stunt people are magnificent," exclaims Stewart. "They've all been doing martial arts since they were children. They're world-champion level, but the thing about them that I really love is that they take the hits. They really hit the ground, so we're not cutting away from a delicate stunt person who doesn't want to get hurt. They're tough, and they're disciplined, and they're trained. They train constantly. I feel the Bulgarian stunt team brought a lot to the action. . . . Rather than cinematic and editorial trickery to do fighting work, we were able to stay in longer shots, and play them literal for what they were, rather than having to cut away from a miss or a punch that didn't connect, or something like that. They brought a lot to it. They really, really did."

The filmmakers wanted to make this battle seem as realistic as possible. "She doesn't deal with any magic," says Daley of Holga. "The only thing that's semi-magical is her barbarian rage, which is this thing that a barbarian can tap into that suddenly increases their strength and gives them almost superhuman skills. There are a few times when she knocks people away to an impossible degree, but we really wanted to ground her fighting style and make it feel as real and tangible as we could."

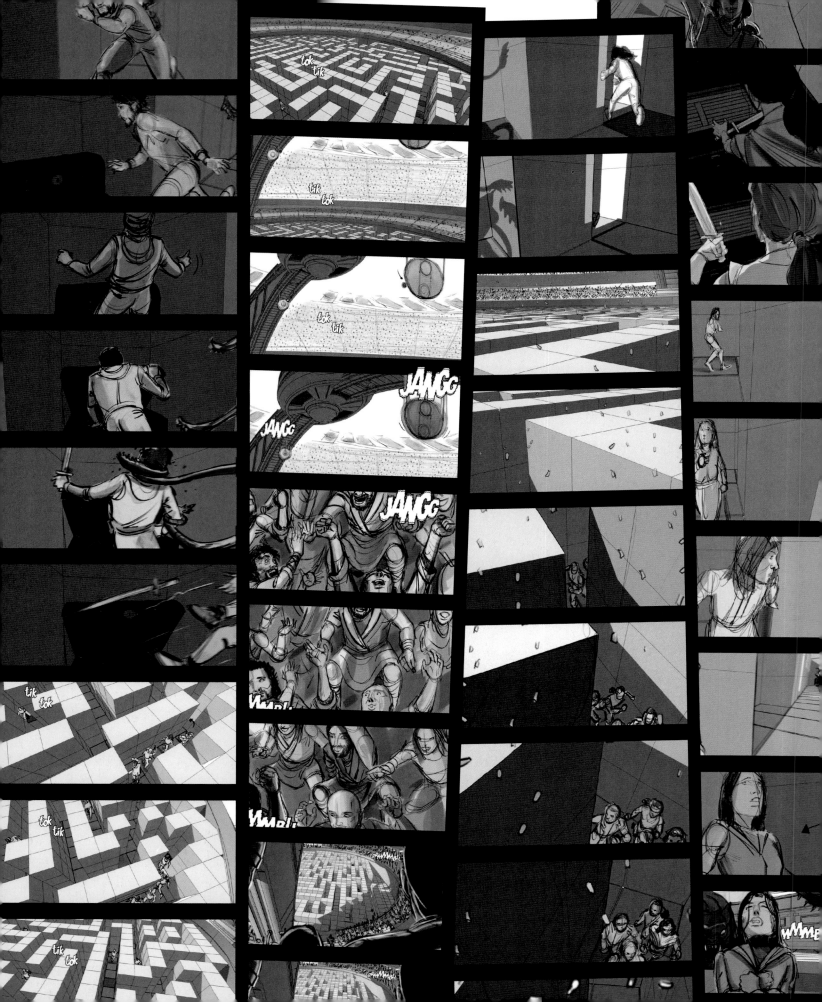

NEVERWINTER ARENA ESCAPE

The return of the High Sun Games has arrived. The event, once stopped for being too brutal, is back on in Neverwinter, and the people couldn't be more thrilled. "We captured a really big scene there with tons and tons of extras all feeling the excitement of the Neverwinter games coming into fruition," states Latcham. "You see banners, and guards, and people out barbecuing and having fun and playing games with one another, and you start to feel the hustle and bustle of the place."

"We had 'game-day' style vendors selling flags, souvenirs featuring the monsters, flower crowns, [and] drinks," recalls Moore. "For the stalls themselves, we sourced some really interesting carved pillars and posts from India, and designed the stalls around what we had found. These were actually designed by our amazing local set-dec assistant Sian, who managed to design a whole set in between looking after our whole team."

As you head toward the arena's gate, artwork informs the spectators of what kinds of beasts lurk inside. "There's a lot of these colorful sort of teal and orange tile work, which is again a nod to the lore where we can feature, let's say, the hook horror or this displacer beast without actually having them in the movie," says Chan. "My inspiration came from a boxing match and seeing Conor McGregor's face on a giant poster, so this is my homage to that. It's a big fight." Hovering high above the arena is a hot-air balloon with Forge Fitzwilliam's face emblazoned on its envelope—the balloon part of the flying machine. As commoners begin to fill the stadium's seats, dignitaries sit high above the arena's center, placing bets with a broker from the comfort of their luxury box. "For the luxury box, we really wanted to create the D&D version of a private Vegas casino," Moore states. "The table was designed by one of the art department's concept artists, and then made by our team of modelmakers. This was particularly challenging as it was at the point in the job where around 90 percent of their team were isolating due to COVID. We designed a game based on the guests being able to place bets on how each contestant might meet their end."

"It is an event that brings the entirety of Faerûn together," Latcham explains of the High Sun Games. "It's

a series of challenges. The one that we get to really experience is a giant maze, and what you come to find out is it's a brutal, brutal world where maybe someone can survive, but mostly it's a bit of a blood sport that gives the people of Neverwinter something to show up and cheer for."

Mazes and Monsters

When the adventuring party is caught sneaking around in Castle Never, they are thrown into the arena as unwilling contestants. "Our heroes are taken and captured, and they're put into a maze, which is in this vast arena," says Snow. "We were able to build a section of the maze and the heroes really run through it. But we can't really build a whole area. It's a massive arena in Neverwinter. So, you know, Ray[mond] Chan built us an exterior of the arena so we can see the people going in. We built a section of bleachers for the people to sit, and then we built a bit of the playing field, so basically, it's a little bit like a game the heroes are in. It goes back to the fact that this is DUNGEONS & DRAGONS, and the heroes [are] on this playing field and suddenly all these pillars rise up and make a maze, and in that maze is a deadly creature—or a couple of deadly creatures, actually. So, they have to evade death and they have [to] race through and work out how to escape somehow. So, in that case, if the pillar's moving, it's going to be computer graphics. If it's not moving, [I ask myself] can it be set? [If] yes, great, but we can't make enough of the maze to cover the whole movie—but we make enough that when we make our computer graphics, we have a very good piece of set to match to."

This arena sequence was almost something else entirely. "The initial concept for the arena maze wasn't a maze at all," recalls Cordova. "In fact, the original concept was a pyramid, and our heroes' initial goal was to reach the cage at the top. During pre-production John and Jonathan came up with the idea to change it into a maze, which helped make the threat of the displacer beast greater so it could hunt its victims in

enclosed quarters instead of out in the open. The way the walls raise and recede in sections were always part of the ticking-time-bomb aspect of the story, and were designed to feel both mechanical and magical in nature. Our ILM supervisor, Scott Benza, and his team at ILM had the unique challenge of building arena columns that rise and fall, all with unique animation and weight so it didn't feel too uniformly mechanical or modern."

Various creatures roam the labyrinth, confronting any heroes who happen to cross their paths. "We get to see a bunch of different classic kind of beasts that we would see from the lore," says Latcham. "We have some mimic monsters. We have a gelatinous cube. We have a displacer beast. So, we get to see this whole little array of the fun stuff that we want to see from the game." Like the owlbear transformation sequence, and the castle escape sequence, stunt performers were utilized to act as placeholders for visual effects. "We have our proxy stunt performers playing the characters, and so we know when the displacer beast is chasing them," adds Snow.

Additional creatures—like kruthiks and rust monsters—almost made it into the arena. "When it comes to VFX, every monster that you create digitally has a great cost attached to it," explains Goldstein. "We had envisioned multiple monsters at certain places and we had to

pick our favorites because it was a difference of hundreds of thousands of dollars to [include] all the monsters we wanted because there's so many great ones."

Edgin and his crew aren't the only competitors in the arena. "We meet two adventuring parties that are also contestants in the maze," says Latcham. "There are contestants made up of the classics '80s animated show, which I think is going to be a lot of fun for a lot of fans. You see Hank, you see Diana, you're seeing Presto, you see Bobby—you see the whole gang. They're kind of together, this '80s gang that you've watched on TV as a kid growing up, and that's a bit of a nostalgia blast. And then, for today's kind of modern D&D player, there's an adventuring party that feels like the most up-to-date, [fifth-edition], full-blown adventuring party with the dragonborn, and it's a very cool group of people as well. So, we have these two parties both rising up on these platforms. They all intended to be in the games, unlike our heroes who've been thrown into the games as a last-minute bid to try to save their lives."

"The arena maze is one of my favorite sequences," exclaims Cordova. "It showcases all the fun elements you'd expect from a D&D movie—creatures, loot, obstacles, and your party having to think outside of the box, or in this case inside a gel cube, to solve a problem."

DON'T I KNOW YOU?

Edgin's party formed so they could reunite with Kira and steal an essential item back from Forge, but these things rarely go to plan. They didn't exactly sign up for the High Sun Games, but as it turns out, the world of DUNGEONS & DRAGONS is full of adventurers ready to band together and pursue their quests. Two of these parties have also entered the High Sun Games . . . and one team looks *very* familiar. Keen-eyed fans of the DUNGEONS & DRAGONS animated series will be able to spot Hank, Eric, Diana, Presto, Sheila, and Bobby in their iconic 80s-style garb within the arena.

SHEILA

HANK

PRESTO

ERIC

DIANA

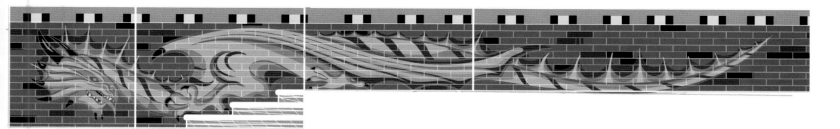

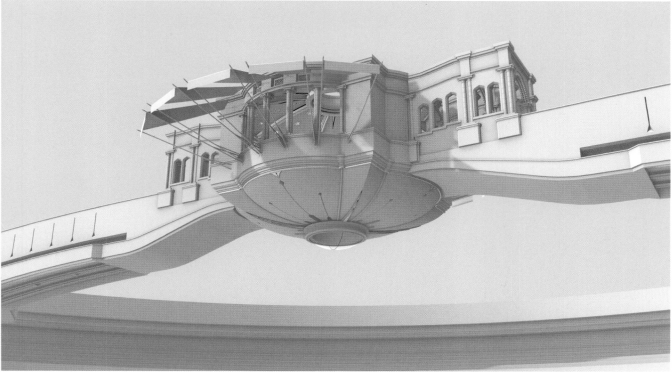

FINAL BATTLE

The High Sun Games are currently in progress, with the crowd cheering at the spectacle, but observant audiences may notice that not all is well in Neverwinter. "So we're not really sure why the games are happening, but we come to suspect, over the course of the film, that this gathering of people might be not quite what it's billed as—it might not be quite what we think it's going to be," says Latcham. "The real plan for the games is actually more to do with Sofina. Because there's something that happened in Thay hundreds of years ago that she wants to replicate, and it requires a lot of people, and it needs all the people in one spot."

Sofina, holding the engraved horn stolen from Korinn's Keep a year earlier, begins to perform the *beckoning death* spell. Red tendrils pour out from the horn's base and spread across the sky. The entire crowd at the game is in danger. Edgin's adventuring party, having escaped the arena and already beginning to sail out into the Sea of Swords, notices the danger overhead. They know they must do something to stop Sofina. The group turns around and races back toward Neverwinter, hoping they won't be too late. "I built a slide deck presentation . . . on what is magic in DUNGEONS & DRAGONS, and I knew that John and Jonathan were keen on everything being real—anchoring things in reality," recalls Snow. "So, part of the approach was to look at special-effects techniques that we could have Sam Conway's team help us out with. Like, we looked at different chemical reactions, different types of smoke, and for something, like, at the end of the film, there's the tentacles of red death, the crimson tendrils, we looked at what chemical reactions look interesting, and so, we latched on to something that we would anchor to that was real, so that was really the thing."

Defeating the Wizards

The team confronts Sofina in the plaza outside of the arena, and a battle ensues. "Ray Chan, our production designer, has done an incredible job of building this place," says Latcham. "You feel like you're in a real place. It looks real. It smells real. I mean, it's crazy how authentic this place feels—but with all the advantages of being on a back lot so we can blow the place to hell and back, and

we can have big explosions, and big pyro, and big effects, and really do something cool." As the plaza would be used for filming both before and during the battle, many factors needed to be considered during the set's construction. "I needed to make sure that the things like the meteor [spell's] impacts, these things that needed to be in the set floor before we even began filming [were] in there [for the] normal, pristine set," says Conway. "I needed to make sure that they all knew what we were doing [for special effects]. . . . And then, obviously, there's all that stunt interaction, with them flying around, and bits and pieces happening. So that was important to get as much information. And, of course, that was the sequence that was forever changing—forever changing—so there were quite a few made-up moments from the day."

The battle leaves the city in ruins. To create some of the damage when destroying a storefront, the filmmakers once again got creative to bring the scene to life. "So, what is smashing the market store?" asks Conway. "I've got a Mini Cooper—a little Mini Cooper—and I race it around the carport. And I thought, 'That's great! I'll get that.' So, I used the Mini Cooper. We stripped it down and put a cage around it, and all that sort of thing, and painted it blue, and that was what was smashing through the stores."

"The biggest challenge was how to create the market stalls for the arena plaza to look good on camera, but also

be able to be smashed into and destroyed both safely, and in a way that could be repeated quickly," adds Moore. "We used a fair few breakaways and softs, as well as lots of items that could be easily repeated when crushed."

Making sure the battle would edit together seamlessly was a struggle of the sequence. "One of the problems with that final battle was that continuity," recalls Daley. "It was a continuity nightmare because, very often, we would pick up segments of the battle that take place much later, after a bunch of damage to the city was done. So, it was a real collaboration with our visual-effects department as well, in keeping that damage consistent and continuous throughout."

The end of the world may not be on the line, but if the adventuring party fails, there is still much to lose. "The key to the film is the stakes are always boiling over," Latcham reminds. "There is real emotion, and real drama that is driving all of the crazy, ludicrous things that are happening in the movie. And I think that's the thing that is going to keep the audience on the edge of their seats. Because they can laugh, but they know in the back of their brains and in their hearts, the stakes are real. Like, 'I don't know if Edgin's going to make it. I don't know if he gets his daughter back. I don't know if they're going to save the city. I can't tell what's going to happen, or how it's going to unfold, but I'm having a good time finding out.'"

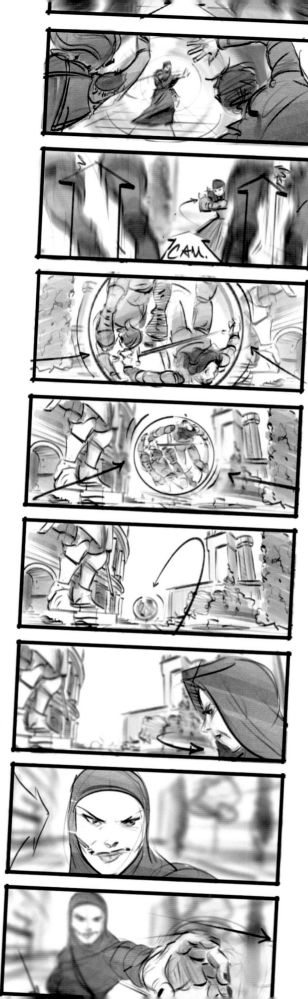

Finishing a story arc does not necessarily mean a campaign is over. Perhaps celebrations for saving the kingdom are interrupted by a party-crashing demigod. Perhaps the king's reward of golden treasure unwittingly includes a cursed idol, transporting the group to a far-off land. Whatever the scenario, with willing players and a creative DM, you can always begin a new and exciting adventure.

AFTERWORD

◆—◆—◆

YOU NEVER REALLY KNOW HOW A MOVIE IS GOING TO DO. Will audiences like it? Will critics embrace it? Will it be the kind of film that people watch over and over again? Or the kind of movie that just sort of comes and goes? These are the questions that can haunt you while you make a film. As a producer, you must separate yourself from these questions and instead focus on making the best movie that you can.

Instead of worrying (or, more likely, while worrying), you spend years of your life collaborating. Working hand-in-hand with a key group of people who show up every day to try and make something that you all, collectively, find utterly delightful. You do this in the hopes that the world will also find the finished movie to be utterly delightful. And maybe, just maybe, you will get lucky and make a movie that audiences love as much as you do. After years of hard work, I'm so thankful and proud to say that *Dungeons & Dragons: Honor Among Thieves* is a movie that I truly love.

Dungeons & Dragons: Honor Among Thieves was handmade with care by a group of tireless and talented filmmakers. This book tells the story of the hundreds of artists, artisans, old-school craftspeople, and high-tech digital wizards that got together in the middle of a global pandemic to try and make something cool. This group's work stretched over continents and involved thousands, likely even hundreds of thousands, of person-hours. It covers a huge swath of disciplines: concept art, storyboards, costume cutting, paint and plaster, pre-viz, leatherwork, stunts, rigging, lighting, camera, prosthetics, set design, hair and makeup, sculpting, food styling, graphic design, digital compositing, special effects, visual effects, helicopter flying, and shipbuilding. The artists in each of these disciplines are among the best in the world at their particular jobs.

A film crew in action is truly a sight to behold. And a film crew working together with creative and financial support from two studios with the sole aim of achieving the very specific vision that was put forth on the page by incredible screenwriters and under the supervision of those same writers as totally fearless directors is a singular experience.

Making this movie was a labor of love, and I truly hope that love comes through to everyone that watches the film. I hope it becomes a movie that lasts. And I also hope that this book will inspire the next generation of writers, directors, cinematographers, artists, artisans, new-school craftspeople, and even higher-tech digital wizards.

See you at the movies.

Jeremy Latcham, producer, p.g.a.
Austin, Texas

Paramount Pictures Corporation: Ralph Bertelle, Denise Cubbins, Jon Gonda, Shari Hanson, Mike Ireland, Stephanie Ito, Risa Kessler, Meg Lewis, and Sabi Lofgren

eOne: Ashley Alexander, Dora Candelaria, Zev Foreman, and Nick Meyer

Wizards of the Coast: Jeremy Jarvis and Nathan Stewart

The producers would like to thank Andrew Pace and Stacey Burns for their help pulling all of the artwork and interviews together.

Special thanks to all the artists who created the concepts and illustrations featured in this book, including Nick Ainsworth, Bryan Andrews, Liam Beck, Alessandro Bertolazzi, Maria Brady, Wes Burt, Lucy Calder, Darrin Denlinger, Oliver Doherty, Janina Eberding, Sean Forsythe, Paul Gerrard, Monty Granito, Wayne Hagg, Glenn Hanz, Tim Hill, George Hull, David Krentz, Jared Krichevsky, Raphael Lubke, Titus Lunter, Dale Mackie, Aidan Monaghan, Jay Oliva, Scott Patton, Manuel Plank-Jorge, April Prime, Raj Rihal, Dean Sherriff, Bodin Sterba, Christopher Swift, Kurt Van Der Basch, Cristina Waltz, Darrell Warner, Simon Webber, and Ivan Weightman.

Character artwork on page 186 by Red Central.
Concept artwork on page 196 designed by yU+co.

Typefaces: Tiamat Condensed and Tiamat Text by Jim Parkinson, Scala Pro and Scala Sans by Martin Majoor for FontFont

Library of Congress Cataloging-in-Publication Data
Names: Roussos, Eleni, author.
Title: The art and making of Dungeons & dragons: honor among thieves / Eleni Roussos.
Description: First edition. | Emeryville : Ten Speed Press, 2023. | Summary: "The official behind-the-scenes companion to Dungeons & Dragons: Honor Among Thieves, featuring cast and crew interviews, photos, and insights about making the film"—Provided by publisher.
Identifiers: LCCN 2022040055 (print) | LCCN 2022040056 (ebook) | ISBN 9781984861863 (hardcover) | ISBN 9781984861870 (ebook)
Subjects: LCSH: Dungeons & dragons: honor among thieves (Motion picture)
Classification: LCC PN1997.2.D865 R68 2023 (print) | LCC PN1997.2.D865 (ebook) | DDC 791.43/72—dc23/eng/20221014
LC record available at https://lccn.loc.gov/2022040055
LC ebook record available at https://lccn.loc.gov/2022040056

Hardcover ISBN: 978-1-9848-6186-3
eBook ISBN: 978-1-9848-6187-0

Printed in Canada

Editor: Shaida Boroumand
Production editors: Doug Ogan, Bridget Sweet
Editorial assistant: Kausaur Fahimuddin
Designer: Debbie Berne
Art director: Betsy Stromberg
Production manager: Dan Myers
Prepress color manager: Jane Chinn
Copyeditor: Robin Slutzky
Proofreaders: Shoshana Seid-Green, Sasha Tropp
Publicist: Lauren Ealy
Marketer: Ashleigh Heaton

10 9 8 7 6 5 4 3 2 1

First Edition

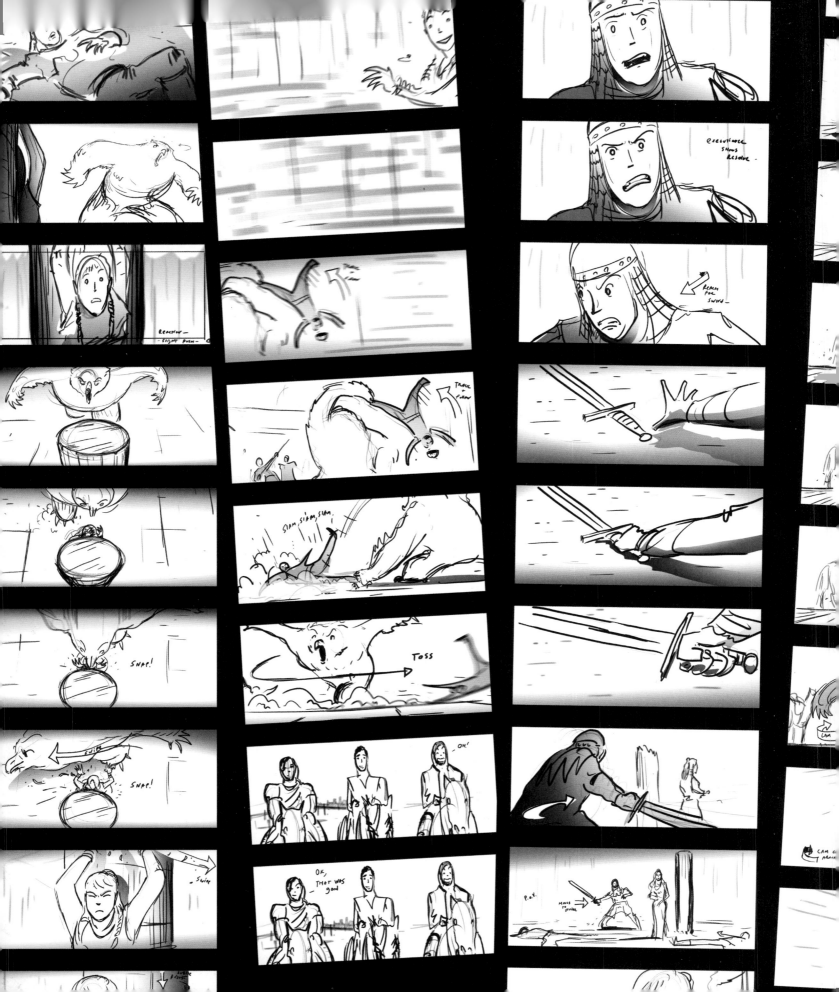